MOOD JOURNAL

Mental Health Tracker

This Book Belongs To

Name :

Phone :

Email :

DATE: _____ S M T W T F S   HOURS SLEPT: _____

MORNING MOOD

😊 🙂 😐 🙁 😟

ENERGY LEVEL
_____
_____
_____

ACTIVITIES

GOAL FOR TODAY...
♡ _____
♡♡ _____
♡♡♡ _____

❀ THREE THINGS I AM GRATEFUL FOR....
1. _____
2. _____
3. _____

FOOD INTAKE
_____
_____
_____

JOURNAL ENTRY/FREE SPACE...

· + ❋ · ★ ❋ o ❋ ✺ ❋ o ❋ ★ · ❋ + ·

EVENING MOOD

😊 🙂 😐 🙁 😟

ENERGY LEVEL
_____
_____
_____

ACTIVITIES

TODAY I WAS ANXIOUS ABOUT...
_____
_____
_____

❀ THREE POSITIVE THINGS ABOUT MY DAY WERE:
1. _____
2. _____
3. _____

FOOD INTAKE
_____
_____
_____
_____

JOURNAL ENTRY/FREE SPACE...

DATE: _____ S M T W T F S   HOURS SLEPT: _____

MORNING MOOD
☺ ☺ ☺ ☹ ☹

ENERGY LEVEL
_____
_____
_____

ACTIVITIES

♡ GOAL FOR TODAY... _____
♡♡ _____
♡♡♡ _____

❀ THREE THINGS I AM GRATEFUL FOR....
1. _____
2. _____
3. _____

FOOD INTAKE
_____
_____
_____
_____

JOURNAL ENTRY/FREE SPACE...

· ✢ ✵ · · ✵ ○ ✳ ☀ ✱ ○ ✳ · ✵ ✢ ·

EVENING MOOD
☺ ☺ ☺ ☹ ☹

ENERGY LEVEL
_____
_____
_____

ACTIVITIES

TODAY I WAS ANXIOUS ABOUT...
_____
_____
_____

❀ THREE POSITIVE THINGS ABOUT MY DAY WERE:
1. _____
2. _____
3. _____

FOOD INTAKE
_____
_____
_____
_____

JOURNAL ENTRY/FREE SPACE...

DATE: _____ S M T W T F S   HOURS SLEPT: _____

MORNING MOOD

😊 🙂 😐 🙁 ☹️

ENERGY LEVEL
_____
_____
_____

ACTIVITIES

GOAL FOR TODAY...
♡ _____
♡♡ _____
♡♡♡ _____

❄ THREE THINGS I AM GRATEFUL FOR....
1. _____
2. _____
3. _____

FOOD INTAKE
_____
_____
_____

JOURNAL ENTRY/FREE SPACE...

· + ✱ · ★ ✱ · ○ ✱ ⚡ ✶ ○ ✱ · ✱ +

EVENING MOOD

😊 🙂 😐 🙁 ☹️

ENERGY LEVEL
_____
_____
_____

ACTIVITIES

TODAY I WAS ANXIOUS ABOUT...
_____
_____
_____

❄ THREE POSITIVE THINGS ABOUT MY DAY WERE:
1. _____
2. _____
3. _____

FOOD INTAKE
_____
_____
_____

JOURNAL ENTRY/FREE SPACE...

DATE: _____ S M T W T F S   HOURS SLEPT: _____

MORNING MOOD
☺ ☺ 😐 ☹ ☹

ENERGY LEVEL
_____
_____
_____

ACTIVITIES

GOAL FOR TODAY...
♡ _____
♡♡ _____
♡♡♡ _____

❀ THREE THINGS I AM GRATEFUL FOR....
1. _____
2. _____
3. _____

FOOD INTAKE
_____
_____
_____
_____

JOURNAL ENTRY/FREE SPACE...

EVENING MOOD
☺ ☺ 😐 ☹ ☹

ENERGY LEVEL
_____
_____
_____

ACTIVITIES

TODAY I WAS ANXIOUS ABOUT...
_____
_____
_____

❀ THREE POSITIVE THINGS ABOUT MY DAY WERE:
1. _____
2. _____
3. _____

FOOD INTAKE
_____
_____
_____
_____

JOURNAL ENTRY/FREE SPACE...

DATE: _____ S M T W T F S   HOURS SLEPT: _____

MORNING MOOD

😀 🙂 😐 🙁 ☹️

ENERGY LEVEL
_____
_____
_____

ACTIVITIES

♡ GOAL FOR TODAY... _____
♡♡ _____
♡♡♡ _____

❀ THREE THINGS I AM GRATEFUL FOR....

1. _____
2. _____
3. _____

FOOD INTAKE
_____
_____
_____

JOURNAL ENTRY/FREE SPACE...

· + ✱ · ✦ ✱ · ✱ ○ ✱ ✺ ✱ ○ ✱ ✦ · ✱ + ·

EVENING MOOD

😀 🙂 😐 🙁 ☹️

ENERGY LEVEL
_____
_____
_____

ACTIVITIES

TODAY I WAS ANXIOUS ABOUT...
_____
_____
_____

❀ THREE POSITIVE THINGS ABOUT MY DAY WERE:

1. _____
2. _____
3. _____

FOOD INTAKE
_____
_____
_____

JOURNAL ENTRY/FREE SPACE...

DATE: _____ S M T W T F S   HOURS SLEPT: _____

MORNING MOOD
😊 🙂 😐 🙁 ☹️

ENERGY LEVEL

ACTIVITIES

♡ GOAL FOR TODAY... _____
♡♡ _____
♡♡♡ _____

❁ THREE THINGS I AM GRATEFUL FOR....
1. _____
2. _____
3. _____

FOOD INTAKE

JOURNAL ENTRY/FREE SPACE...

· + ✷ • ✲ ✱ ○ ✶ ☀ ✹ ○ ✱ ★ • ✷ + ·

EVENING MOOD
😊 🙂 😐 🙁 ☹️

ENERGY LEVEL

ACTIVITIES

TODAY I WAS ANXIOUS ABOUT...
_____
_____

❁ THREE POSITIVE THINGS ABOUT MY DAY WERE:
1. _____
2. _____
3. _____

FOOD INTAKE

JOURNAL ENTRY/FREE SPACE...

DATE: _____ S M T W T F S   HOURS SLEPT: _____

MORNING MOOD

😊 🙂 😐 🙁 😟

ENERGY LEVEL
_____
_____
_____

ACTIVITIES

♡ GOAL FOR TODAY... _____
♡♡ _____
♡♡♡ _____

❋ THREE THINGS I AM GRATEFUL FOR....

1. _____
2. _____
3. _____

FOOD INTAKE
_____
_____
_____

JOURNAL ENTRY/FREE SPACE...

EVENING MOOD

😊 🙂 😐 🙁 😟

ENERGY LEVEL
_____
_____
_____

ACTIVITIES

TODAY I WAS ANXIOUS ABOUT...
_____
_____
_____

❋ THREE POSITIVE THINGS ABOUT MY DAY WERE:

1. _____
2. _____
3. _____

FOOD INTAKE
_____
_____
_____

JOURNAL ENTRY/FREE SPACE...

DATE: ——————— S M T W T F S   HOURS SLEPT: ———————

MORNING MOOD

😀 🙂 😐 🙁 ☹️

ENERGY LEVEL

ACTIVITIES

♡ GOAL FOR TODAY...
♡♡ ————————————————
♡♡♡ ———————————————

❈ THREE THINGS I AM GRATEFUL FOR....

1. _____
2. _____
3. _____

FOOD INTAKE

JOURNAL ENTRY/FREE SPACE...

· + ✳ • ✶ ✳ ○ ✳ ☀ ✳ ○ ✳ ✶ • ✳ + ·

EVENING MOOD

😀 🙂 😐 🙁 ☹️

ENERGY LEVEL

ACTIVITIES

TODAY I WAS ANXIOUS ABOUT...
_____
_____
_____

❈ THREE POSITIVE THINGS ABOUT MY DAY WERE:

1. _____
2. _____
3. _____

FOOD INTAKE

JOURNAL ENTRY/FREE SPACE...

DATE: _____ S M T W T F S   HOURS SLEPT: _____

MORNING MOOD

😊 🙂 😐 🙁 ☹️

ENERGY LEVEL

ACTIVITIES

GOAL FOR TODAY...
♡ _____
♡♡ _____
♡♡♡ _____

❋ THREE THINGS I AM GRATEFUL FOR....

1. _____
2. _____
3. _____

FOOD INTAKE

JOURNAL ENTRY/FREE SPACE...

EVENING MOOD

😊 🙂 😐 🙁 ☹️

ENERGY LEVEL

ACTIVITIES

TODAY I WAS ANXIOUS ABOUT...
_____
_____
_____

❋ THREE POSITIVE THINGS ABOUT MY DAY WERE:

1. _____
2. _____
3. _____

FOOD INTAKE

JOURNAL ENTRY/FREE SPACE...

DATE: _____ S M T W T F S   HOURS SLEPT: _____

MORNING MOOD

😊 🙂 😐 🙁 ☹️

ENERGY LEVEL

ACTIVITIES

GOAL FOR TODAY...
♡ _____
♡♡ _____
♡♡♡ _____

❋ THREE THINGS I AM GRATEFUL FOR....

1. _____
2. _____
3. _____

FOOD INTAKE

JOURNAL ENTRY/FREE SPACE...

· ✶ ❋ · ✱ ❋ ○ ❋ ☀ ❋ ○ ❋ ✱ · ❋ ✶ ·

EVENING MOOD

😊 🙂 😐 🙁 ☹️

ENERGY LEVEL

ACTIVITIES

TODAY I WAS ANXIOUS ABOUT...
_____
_____
_____

❋ THREE POSITIVE THINGS ABOUT MY DAY WERE:

1. _____
2. _____
3. _____

FOOD INTAKE

JOURNAL ENTRY/FREE SPACE...

DATE: _____ S M T W T F S   HOURS SLEPT: _____

MORNING MOOD

ENERGY LEVEL

ACTIVITIES

😊 🙂 😐 🙁 ☹️

GOAL FOR TODAY...
♡ _____
♡♡ _____
♡♡♡ _____

❋ THREE THINGS I AM GRATEFUL FOR....
1. _____
2. _____
3. _____

FOOD INTAKE

JOURNAL ENTRY/FREE SPACE...

_____
_____
_____
_____

· + ❋ • ❋ ❋ ❋ ○ ❋ ☀ ❋ ○ ❋ ❋ • ❋ + ·

EVENING MOOD

ENERGY LEVEL

ACTIVITIES

😊 🙂 😐 🙁 ☹️

TODAY I WAS ANXIOUS ABOUT...
_____
_____
_____

❋ THREE POSITIVE THINGS ABOUT MY DAY WERE:
1. _____
2. _____
3. _____

FOOD INTAKE

JOURNAL ENTRY/FREE SPACE...

_____
_____
_____
_____

DATE: _____ S M T W T F S   HOURS SLEPT: _____

MORNING MOOD
☺ ☺ 😐 ☹ ☹

ENERGY LEVEL
_____
_____
_____

ACTIVITIES

GOAL FOR TODAY...
♡ _____
♡♡ _____
♡♡♡ _____

❀ THREE THINGS I AM GRATEFUL FOR....
1. _____
2. _____
3. _____

FOOD INTAKE
_____
_____
_____

JOURNAL ENTRY/FREE SPACE...

· ✦ ✱ • • ✶ ✱ ○ ✱ ☼ ✶ ○ ✱ ✦ • ✶ ✦ ·

EVENING MOOD
☺ ☺ 😐 ☹ ☹

ENERGY LEVEL
_____
_____
_____

ACTIVITIES

TODAY I WAS ANXIOUS ABOUT...
_____
_____
_____

❀ THREE POSITIVE THINGS ABOUT MY DAY WERE:
1. _____
2. _____
3. _____

FOOD INTAKE
_____
_____
_____
_____

JOURNAL ENTRY/FREE SPACE...

DATE: _____ S M T W T F S   HOURS SLEPT: _____

MORNING MOOD

😊 🙂 😐 🙁 😟

ENERGY LEVEL

ACTIVITIES

♡ GOAL FOR TODAY... _____
♡♡ _____
♡♡♡ _____

❊ THREE THINGS I AM GRATEFUL FOR....

1. _____
2. _____
3. _____

FOOD INTAKE

JOURNAL ENTRY/FREE SPACE...

. + ✱ • ✴ ✱ o ✷ ✺ ✶ o ✱ • ✱ + .

EVENING MOOD

😊 🙂 😐 🙁 😟

ENERGY LEVEL

ACTIVITIES

TODAY I WAS ANXIOUS ABOUT...
_____
_____
_____

❊ THREE POSITIVE THINGS ABOUT MY DAY WERE:

1. _____
2. _____
3. _____

FOOD INTAKE

JOURNAL ENTRY/FREE SPACE...

DATE: _____ S M T W T F S   HOURS SLEPT: _____

MORNING MOOD ☀

☺ ☺ 😐 🙁 ☹

ENERGY LEVEL

ACTIVITIES

♡ GOAL FOR TODAY...
♡♡ _____
♡♡♡ _____

❀ THREE THINGS I AM GRATEFUL FOR....

1. _____
2. _____
3. _____

FOOD INTAKE

JOURNAL ENTRY/FREE SPACE...

· + ✻ • ✱ ✻ ○ ✱ ☀ ✱ ○ ✱ ★ • ✻ + ·

EVENING MOOD 🌙

☺ ☺ 😐 🙁 ☹

ENERGY LEVEL

ACTIVITIES

TODAY I WAS ANXIOUS ABOUT...
_____
_____

❀ THREE POSITIVE THINGS ABOUT MY DAY WERE:

1. _____
2. _____
3. _____

FOOD INTAKE

JOURNAL ENTRY/FREE SPACE...

DATE: _____   S M T W T F S   HOURS SLEPT: _____

MORNING MOOD

😊 😀 😐 ☹️ 😟

ENERGY LEVEL
_____
_____
_____

ACTIVITIES

♡ GOAL FOR TODAY... _____
♡♡ _____
♡♡♡ _____

❀ THREE THINGS I AM GRATEFUL FOR....

1. _____
2. _____
3. _____

FOOD INTAKE
_____
_____
_____

JOURNAL ENTRY/FREE SPACE...

· + ✱ • ✶ ✱ o ✳ ✼ ✱ o ✱ ✶ • ✳ + ·

EVENING MOOD

😊 😀 😐 ☹️ 😟

ENERGY LEVEL
_____
_____
_____

ACTIVITIES

TODAY I WAS ANXIOUS ABOUT...
_____
_____
_____

❀ THREE POSITIVE THINGS ABOUT MY DAY WERE:

1. _____
2. _____
3. _____

FOOD INTAKE
_____
_____
_____
_____

JOURNAL ENTRY/FREE SPACE...

DATE: ——————— S M T W T F S   HOURS SLEPT: ———————

MORNING MOOD

☺ ☺ 😐 ☹ ☹

ENERGY LEVEL

ACTIVITIES

GOAL FOR TODAY...
♡ _____
♡♡ _____
♡♡♡ _____

❀ THREE THINGS I AM GRATEFUL FOR....
1. _____
2. _____
3. _____

FOOD INTAKE

JOURNAL ENTRY/FREE SPACE...

· + ✱ · ✱ ✱ o ✱ ※ ✱ o ✱ ★ · ✱ +·

EVENING MOOD

☺ ☺ 😐 ☹ ☹

ENERGY LEVEL

ACTIVITIES

TODAY I WAS ANXIOUS ABOUT...
_____
_____

❀ THREE POSITIVE THINGS ABOUT MY DAY WERE:
1. _____
2. _____
3. _____

FOOD INTAKE

JOURNAL ENTRY/FREE SPACE...

DATE: _____ S M T W T F S   HOURS SLEPT: _____

MORNING MOOD
😊 😀 😐 ☹️ 😞

ENERGY LEVEL
_____
_____
_____

ACTIVITIES

♡ GOAL FOR TODAY... _____
♡♡ _____
♡♡♡ _____

❋ THREE THINGS I AM GRATEFUL FOR....

1. _____
2. _____
3. _____

FOOD INTAKE
_____
_____
_____
_____

JOURNAL ENTRY/FREE SPACE...

EVENING MOOD
😊 😀 😐 ☹️ 😞

ENERGY LEVEL
_____
_____
_____

ACTIVITIES

TODAY I WAS ANXIOUS ABOUT...
_____
_____
_____

❋ THREE POSITIVE THINGS ABOUT MY DAY WERE:

1. _____
2. _____
3. _____

FOOD INTAKE
_____
_____
_____
_____

JOURNAL ENTRY/FREE SPACE...

DATE: _____ S M T W T F S   HOURS SLEPT: _____

MORNING MOOD
☺ ☺ 😐 ☹ ☹

ENERGY LEVEL

ACTIVITIES

GOAL FOR TODAY...
♡ _____
♡♡ _____
♡♡♡ _____

❋ THREE THINGS I AM GRATEFUL FOR....
1. _____
2. _____
3. _____

FOOD INTAKE

JOURNAL ENTRY/FREE SPACE...

· ✦ ❋ · · ✱ ❋ o ❋ ☀ ✶ o ❋ ✱ · ❋ ✦ ·

EVENING MOOD
☺ ☺ 😐 ☹ ☹

ENERGY LEVEL

ACTIVITIES

TODAY I WAS ANXIOUS ABOUT...
_____
_____
_____

❋ THREE POSITIVE THINGS ABOUT MY DAY WERE:
1. _____
2. _____
3. _____

FOOD INTAKE

JOURNAL ENTRY/FREE SPACE...

DATE: _____ S M T W T F S   HOURS SLEPT: _____

MORNING MOOD

😊 😊 😐 ☹️ 😣

ENERGY LEVEL

ACTIVITIES

GOAL FOR TODAY...
♡ _____
♡♡ _____
♡♡♡ _____

❀ THREE THINGS I AM GRATEFUL FOR....

1. _____
2. _____
3. _____

FOOD INTAKE

JOURNAL ENTRY/FREE SPACE...

EVENING MOOD

😊 😊 😐 ☹️ 😣

ENERGY LEVEL

ACTIVITIES

TODAY I WAS ANXIOUS ABOUT...
_____
_____

❀ THREE POSITIVE THINGS ABOUT MY DAY WERE:

1. _____
2. _____
3. _____

FOOD INTAKE

JOURNAL ENTRY/FREE SPACE...

DATE: _____ S M T W T F S   HOURS SLEPT: _____

MORNING MOOD
😊 🙂 😐 🙁 ☹️

ENERGY LEVEL
_____
_____
_____

ACTIVITIES

GOAL FOR TODAY...
♡ _____
♡♡ _____
♡♡♡ _____

❋ THREE THINGS I AM GRATEFUL FOR....
1. _____
2. _____
3. _____

FOOD INTAKE
_____
_____
_____
_____

JOURNAL ENTRY/FREE SPACE...

· + ❋ · ❋ ✳ ○ ❋ ☀ ✳ ○ ✳ ❋ · ❋ ✚ ·

EVENING MOOD
😊 🙂 😐 🙁 ☹️

ENERGY LEVEL
_____
_____
_____

ACTIVITIES

TODAY I WAS ANXIOUS ABOUT...
_____
_____
_____

❋ THREE POSITIVE THINGS ABOUT MY DAY WERE:
1. _____
2. _____
3. _____

FOOD INTAKE
_____
_____
_____
_____

JOURNAL ENTRY/FREE SPACE...

DATE: _____ S M T W T F S   HOURS SLEPT: _____

MORNING MOOD
😊 🙂 😐 🙁 😟

ENERGY LEVEL
_____
_____
_____

ACTIVITIES

♡ GOAL FOR TODAY...
♡♡ _____
♡♡♡ _____

❋ THREE THINGS I AM GRATEFUL FOR....
1. _____
2. _____
3. _____

FOOD INTAKE
_____
_____
_____

JOURNAL ENTRY/FREE SPACE...

· + ✱ • ★ ✱ ○ ✳ ☀ ✶ ○ ✱ ★ • ✱ + ·

EVENING MOOD
😊 🙂 😐 🙁 😟

ENERGY LEVEL
_____
_____
_____

ACTIVITIES

TODAY I WAS ANXIOUS ABOUT...
_____
_____
_____

❋ THREE POSITIVE THINGS ABOUT MY DAY WERE:
1. _____
2. _____
3. _____

FOOD INTAKE
_____
_____
_____
_____

JOURNAL ENTRY/FREE SPACE...

DATE: _____ S M T W T F S   HOURS SLEPT: _____

MORNING MOOD

☺ ☺ 😐 ☹ ☹

ENERGY LEVEL

ACTIVITIES

GOAL FOR TODAY...
♡ _____
♡♡ _____
♡♡♡ _____

❀ THREE THINGS I AM GRATEFUL FOR....
1. _____
2. _____
3. _____

FOOD INTAKE

JOURNAL ENTRY/FREE SPACE...

· + ✳ • ✱ ✶ o ✱ ✵ ✱ o ✱ ✺ • ✱ ✢ ·

EVENING MOOD

☺ ☺ 😐 ☹ ☹

ENERGY LEVEL

ACTIVITIES

TODAY I WAS ANXIOUS ABOUT...
_____
_____

❀ THREE POSITIVE THINGS ABOUT MY DAY WERE:
1. _____
2. _____
3. _____

FOOD INTAKE

JOURNAL ENTRY/FREE SPACE...

DATE: _____ S M T W T F S   HOURS SLEPT: _____

MORNING MOOD

😊 🙂 😐 🙁 😣

ENERGY LEVEL
_____
_____
_____

ACTIVITIES

♡ GOAL FOR TODAY... _____
♡♡ _____
♡♡♡ _____

❋ THREE THINGS I AM GRATEFUL FOR....

1. _____
2. _____
3. _____

FOOD INTAKE
_____
_____
_____
_____

JOURNAL ENTRY/FREE SPACE...

· ✦ ❋ · ✺ ❋ ∘ ❋ ≋ ✶ ∘ ❋ ✦ · ❋ ✦ ·

EVENING MOOD

😊 🙂 😐 🙁 😣

ENERGY LEVEL
_____
_____
_____

ACTIVITIES

TODAY I WAS ANXIOUS ABOUT...
_____
_____
_____

❋ THREE POSITIVE THINGS ABOUT MY DAY WERE:

1. _____
2. _____
3. _____

FOOD INTAKE
_____
_____
_____
_____

JOURNAL ENTRY/FREE SPACE...

DATE: _____ S M T W T F S   HOURS SLEPT: _____

MORNING MOOD

😃 😊 😐 🙁 ☹️

ENERGY LEVEL

_____
_____
_____

ACTIVITIES

GOAL FOR TODAY...
♡ _____
♡♡ _____
♡♡♡ _____

❁ THREE THINGS I AM GRATEFUL FOR....

1. _____
2. _____
3. _____

FOOD INTAKE

_____
_____
_____
_____

JOURNAL ENTRY/FREE SPACE...

· + ✳ • ✱ ✻ ○ ✷ ☀ ✶ ○ ✱ ★ • ✻ ✢ ·

EVENING MOOD

😃 😊 😐 🙁 ☹️

ENERGY LEVEL

_____
_____
_____

ACTIVITIES

TODAY I WAS ANXIOUS ABOUT...
_____
_____
_____

❁ THREE POSITIVE THINGS ABOUT MY DAY WERE:

1. _____
2. _____
3. _____

FOOD INTAKE

_____
_____
_____
_____

JOURNAL ENTRY/FREE SPACE...

DATE: _____ S M T W T F S   HOURS SLEPT: _____

MORNING MOOD

😊 🙂 😐 🙁 😟

ENERGY LEVEL

ACTIVITIES

♡ GOAL FOR TODAY...
♡♡ _____
♡♡♡ _____

❋ THREE THINGS I AM GRATEFUL FOR....

1. _____
2. _____
3. _____

FOOD INTAKE

JOURNAL ENTRY/FREE SPACE...

· ✦ ✳ · ✵ ✳ ○ ✳ ✺ ✱ ○ ✳ ✦ · ✳ ✦ ·

EVENING MOOD

😊 🙂 😐 🙁 😟

ENERGY LEVEL

ACTIVITIES

TODAY I WAS ANXIOUS ABOUT...
_____
_____

❋ THREE POSITIVE THINGS ABOUT MY DAY WERE:

1. _____
2. _____
3. _____

FOOD INTAKE

JOURNAL ENTRY/FREE SPACE...

DATE: _____ S M T W T F S   HOURS SLEPT: _____

MORNING MOOD

😊 🙂 😐 🙁 ☹️

ENERGY LEVEL

ACTIVITIES

GOAL FOR TODAY...
♡ _____
♡♡ _____
♡♡♡ _____

❀ THREE THINGS I AM GRATEFUL FOR....
1. _____
2. _____
3. _____

FOOD INTAKE

JOURNAL ENTRY/FREE SPACE...

· + ✳ · · ✶ ✳ ○ ✳ ✺ ✷ ○ ✳ ✶ · ✳ ✦ ·

EVENING MOOD

😊 🙂 😐 🙁 ☹️

ENERGY LEVEL

ACTIVITIES

TODAY I WAS ANXIOUS ABOUT...
_____
_____
_____

❀ THREE POSITIVE THINGS ABOUT MY DAY WERE:
1. _____
2. _____
3. _____

FOOD INTAKE

JOURNAL ENTRY/FREE SPACE...

DATE: _____ S M T W T F S   HOURS SLEPT: _____

MORNING MOOD

😊 😃 😐 🙁 😟

ENERGY LEVEL
_____
_____
_____

ACTIVITIES

GOAL FOR TODAY...
♡ _____
♡♡ _____
♡♡♡ _____

❋ THREE THINGS I AM GRATEFUL FOR....
1. _____
2. _____
3. _____

FOOD INTAKE
_____
_____
_____

JOURNAL ENTRY/FREE SPACE...

· + ✱ · ✦ ✱ ○ ✱ ✺ ✹ ○ ✱ • ✱ + ·

EVENING MOOD

😊 😃 😐 🙁 😟

ENERGY LEVEL
_____
_____
_____

ACTIVITIES

TODAY I WAS ANXIOUS ABOUT...
_____
_____
_____

❋ THREE POSITIVE THINGS ABOUT MY DAY WERE:
1. _____
2. _____
3. _____

FOOD INTAKE
_____
_____
_____

JOURNAL ENTRY/FREE SPACE...

DATE: _____ S M T W T F S   HOURS SLEPT: _____

MORNING MOOD

😊 🙂 😐 🙁 ☹️

ENERGY LEVEL
_____
_____
_____

ACTIVITIES

GOAL FOR TODAY...
♡ _____
♡♡ _____
♡♡♡ _____

❀ THREE THINGS I AM GRATEFUL FOR....
1. _____
2. _____
3. _____

FOOD INTAKE
_____
_____
_____
_____

JOURNAL ENTRY/FREE SPACE...

· ✛ ✱ · • ★ ✱ ○ ✳ ☀ ✳ ○ ✱ ★ • ✱ ✛ ·

EVENING MOOD

😊 🙂 😐 🙁 ☹️

ENERGY LEVEL
_____
_____
_____

ACTIVITIES

TODAY I WAS ANXIOUS ABOUT...
_____
_____

❀ THREE POSITIVE THINGS ABOUT MY DAY WERE:
1. _____
2. _____
3. _____

FOOD INTAKE
_____
_____
_____
_____
_____

JOURNAL ENTRY/FREE SPACE...

DATE: _____ S M T W T F S   HOURS SLEPT: _____

MORNING MOOD

😊 🙂 😐 🙁 😞

ENERGY LEVEL

ACTIVITIES

♡ GOAL FOR TODAY...
♡♡ _____
♡♡♡ _____

❋ THREE THINGS I AM GRATEFUL FOR....

1. _____
2. _____
3. _____

FOOD INTAKE

JOURNAL ENTRY/FREE SPACE...

· + ✳ • ★ ✳ o ✱ ✺ ✱ o ✳ ★ • ✳ + ·

EVENING MOOD

😊 🙂 😐 🙁 😞

ENERGY LEVEL

ACTIVITIES

TODAY I WAS ANXIOUS ABOUT...
_____
_____

❋ THREE POSITIVE THINGS ABOUT MY DAY WERE:

1. _____
2. _____
3. _____

FOOD INTAKE

JOURNAL ENTRY/FREE SPACE...

DATE: _____ S M T W T F S   HOURS SLEPT: _____

MORNING MOOD
😊 🙂 😐 🙁 ☹️

ENERGY LEVEL

ACTIVITIES

GOAL FOR TODAY...
♡ _____
♡♡ _____
♡♡♡ _____

❀ THREE THINGS I AM GRATEFUL FOR....
1. _____
2. _____
3. _____

FOOD INTAKE

JOURNAL ENTRY/FREE SPACE...

· ✢ ✳ · ✱ ✳ ○ ✳ ☀ ✶ ○ ✱ ✦ · ✱ ✢ ·

EVENING MOOD
😊 🙂 😐 🙁 ☹️

ENERGY LEVEL

ACTIVITIES

TODAY I WAS ANXIOUS ABOUT...
_____
_____
_____

❀ THREE POSITIVE THINGS ABOUT MY DAY WERE:
1. _____
2. _____
3. _____

FOOD INTAKE

JOURNAL ENTRY/FREE SPACE...

DATE: _____ S M T W T F S   HOURS SLEPT: _____

MORNING MOOD

😊 🙂 😐 🙁 ☹️

ENERGY LEVEL

ACTIVITIES

♡ GOAL FOR TODAY... _____
♡♡ _____
♡♡♡ _____

❋ THREE THINGS I AM GRATEFUL FOR....

1. _____
2. _____
3. _____

FOOD INTAKE

JOURNAL ENTRY/FREE SPACE...

· + ✳ · ✦ ✳ ○ ✳ ☀ ✳ ○ ✳ ✦ · ✳ + ·

EVENING MOOD

😊 🙂 😐 🙁 ☹️

ENERGY LEVEL

ACTIVITIES

TODAY I WAS ANXIOUS ABOUT...
_____
_____
_____

❋ THREE POSITIVE THINGS ABOUT MY DAY WERE:

1. _____
2. _____
3. _____

FOOD INTAKE

JOURNAL ENTRY/FREE SPACE...

DATE: _____ S M T W T F S   HOURS SLEPT: _____

MORNING MOOD
😀 🙂 😐 🙁 ☹️

ENERGY LEVEL
_____
_____
_____

ACTIVITIES

♡ GOAL FOR TODAY... _____
♡♡ _____
♡♡♡ _____

❀ THREE THINGS I AM GRATEFUL FOR....
1. _____
2. _____
3. _____

FOOD INTAKE
_____
_____
_____
_____

JOURNAL ENTRY/FREE SPACE...

· ✦ ✳ · · ✳ ○ ✶ ☀ ✳ ○ ✶ ★ · ✳ ✦ ·

EVENING MOOD
😀 🙂 😐 🙁 ☹️

ENERGY LEVEL
_____
_____
_____

ACTIVITIES

TODAY I WAS ANXIOUS ABOUT...
_____
_____
_____

❀ THREE POSITIVE THINGS ABOUT MY DAY WERE:
1. _____
2. _____
3. _____

FOOD INTAKE
_____
_____
_____
_____

JOURNAL ENTRY/FREE SPACE...

DATE: _____ S M T W T F S   HOURS SLEPT: _____

MORNING MOOD

😀 🙂 😐 🙁 😞

ENERGY LEVEL
_____
_____
_____

ACTIVITIES

♡ GOAL FOR TODAY...
_____
♡♡ _____
♡♡♡ _____

❁ THREE THINGS I AM GRATEFUL FOR....

1. _____
2. _____
3. _____

FOOD INTAKE
_____
_____
_____

JOURNAL ENTRY/FREE SPACE...

· + ✱ • ★ ✳ ○ ✱ ☀ ✱ ○ ✱ ★ • ✱ + ·

EVENING MOOD

😀 🙂 😐 🙁 😞

ENERGY LEVEL
_____
_____
_____

ACTIVITIES

TODAY I WAS ANXIOUS ABOUT...
_____
_____
_____

❁ THREE POSITIVE THINGS ABOUT MY DAY WERE:

1. _____
2. _____
3. _____

FOOD INTAKE
_____
_____
_____
_____

JOURNAL ENTRY/FREE SPACE...

DATE: _____ S M T W T F S   HOURS SLEPT: _____

MORNING MOOD
☺ ☺ 😐 ☹ ☹

ENERGY LEVEL
_____
_____
_____

ACTIVITIES

GOAL FOR TODAY...
♡ _____
♡♡ _____
♡♡♡ _____

❁ THREE THINGS I AM GRATEFUL FOR....
1. _____
2. _____
3. _____

FOOD INTAKE
_____
_____
_____
_____

JOURNAL ENTRY/FREE SPACE...

· + ✳ · ✳ ✳ o ✳ ☀ ✱ o ✳ ✱ · ✳ ✦ ·

EVENING MOOD
☺ ☺ 😐 ☹ ☹

ENERGY LEVEL
_____
_____
_____

ACTIVITIES

TODAY I WAS ANXIOUS ABOUT...
_____
_____
_____

❁ THREE POSITIVE THINGS ABOUT MY DAY WERE:
1. _____
2. _____
3. _____

FOOD INTAKE
_____
_____
_____
_____

JOURNAL ENTRY/FREE SPACE...

DATE: _____ S M T W T F S   HOURS SLEPT: _____

MORNING MOOD

😊 🙂 😐 🙁 😟

ENERGY LEVEL
_____
_____
_____

ACTIVITIES

♡ GOAL FOR TODAY...
♡♡ _____
♡♡♡ _____

❋ THREE THINGS I AM GRATEFUL FOR....

1. _____
2. _____
3. _____

FOOD INTAKE
_____
_____
_____

JOURNAL ENTRY/FREE SPACE...

EVENING MOOD

😊 🙂 😐 🙁 😟

ENERGY LEVEL
_____
_____
_____

ACTIVITIES

TODAY I WAS ANXIOUS ABOUT...
_____
_____
_____

❋ THREE POSITIVE THINGS ABOUT MY DAY WERE:

1. _____
2. _____
3. _____

FOOD INTAKE
_____
_____
_____
_____

JOURNAL ENTRY/FREE SPACE...

DATE: —————— S M T W T F S   HOURS SLEPT: ——————

MORNING MOOD

😊 😊 😐 🙁 ☹️

ENERGY LEVEL

ACTIVITIES

GOAL FOR TODAY...
♡ _____
♡♡ _____
♡♡♡ _____

❋ THREE THINGS I AM GRATEFUL FOR....
1. _____
2. _____
3. _____

FOOD INTAKE

JOURNAL ENTRY/FREE SPACE...

· ✦ ❋ · ✱ ✺ ○ ✱ ☀ ✱ ○ ✱ ✦ · ❋ ✦ ·

EVENING MOOD

😊 😊 😐 🙁 ☹️

ENERGY LEVEL

ACTIVITIES

TODAY I WAS ANXIOUS ABOUT...
_____
_____
_____

❋ THREE POSITIVE THINGS ABOUT MY DAY WERE:
1. _____
2. _____
3. _____

FOOD INTAKE

JOURNAL ENTRY/FREE SPACE...

DATE: _____ S M T W T F S   HOURS SLEPT: _____

MORNING MOOD

😀 🙂 😐 🙁 😟

ENERGY LEVEL
_____
_____
_____

ACTIVITIES

GOAL FOR TODAY...
♡ _____
♡♡ _____
♡♡♡ _____

❋ THREE THINGS I AM GRATEFUL FOR....

1. _____
2. _____
3. _____

FOOD INTAKE
_____
_____
_____

JOURNAL ENTRY/FREE SPACE...

· ✦ ✱ • ✸ ✱ ○ ✱ ✺ ✶ ○ ✱ ✦ • ✱ ✦ ·

EVENING MOOD

😀 🙂 😐 🙁 😟

ENERGY LEVEL
_____
_____
_____

ACTIVITIES

TODAY I WAS ANXIOUS ABOUT...
_____
_____
_____

❋ THREE POSITIVE THINGS ABOUT MY DAY WERE:

1. _____
2. _____
3. _____

FOOD INTAKE
_____
_____
_____
_____

JOURNAL ENTRY/FREE SPACE...

DATE: _____ S M T W T F S   HOURS SLEPT: _____

MORNING MOOD

☺ ☺ ☺ ☹ ☹

ENERGY LEVEL

ACTIVITIES

GOAL FOR TODAY...
♡ _____
♡♡ _____
♡♡♡ _____

❊ THREE THINGS I AM GRATEFUL FOR....
1. _____
2. _____
3. _____

FOOD INTAKE

JOURNAL ENTRY/FREE SPACE...

· ✢ ✱ · ✦ ✱ ○ ✱ ☀ ✱ ○ ✱ ✦ · ✱ ✢ ·

EVENING MOOD

☺ ☺ ☺ ☹ ☹

ENERGY LEVEL

ACTIVITIES

TODAY I WAS ANXIOUS ABOUT...
_____
_____
_____

❊ THREE POSITIVE THINGS ABOUT MY DAY WERE:
1. _____
2. _____
3. _____

FOOD INTAKE

JOURNAL ENTRY/FREE SPACE...

DATE: _____ S M T W T F S   HOURS SLEPT: _____

MORNING MOOD

😊 🙂 😐 🙁 ☹️

ENERGY LEVEL

ACTIVITIES

♡ GOAL FOR TODAY... _____
♡♡ _____
♡♡♡ _____

❀ THREE THINGS I AM GRATEFUL FOR....

1. _____
2. _____
3. _____

FOOD INTAKE

JOURNAL ENTRY/FREE SPACE...

· + ✳ · ✱ ✶ ✳ ☀ ✶ ○ ✱ ✦ · ✳ + ·

EVENING MOOD

😊 🙂 😐 🙁 ☹️

ENERGY LEVEL

ACTIVITIES

TODAY I WAS ANXIOUS ABOUT...
_____
_____

❀ THREE POSITIVE THINGS ABOUT MY DAY WERE:

1. _____
2. _____
3. _____

FOOD INTAKE

JOURNAL ENTRY/FREE SPACE...

DATE: ——————— S M T W T F S   HOURS SLEPT: ———————

MORNING MOOD
😀 🙂 😐 🙁 ☹️

ENERGY LEVEL

ACTIVITIES

GOAL FOR TODAY...
♡ _____
♡♡ _____
♡♡♡ _____

❀ THREE THINGS I AM GRATEFUL FOR....
1. _____
2. _____
3. _____

FOOD INTAKE

JOURNAL ENTRY/FREE SPACE...

· ✢ ✳ · ✦ ✱ ○ ✳ ☀ ✳ ○ ✱ ✦ · ✳ ✢ ·

EVENING MOOD
😀 🙂 😐 🙁 ☹️

ENERGY LEVEL

ACTIVITIES

TODAY I WAS ANXIOUS ABOUT...
_____
_____

❀ THREE POSITIVE THINGS ABOUT MY DAY WERE:
1. _____
2. _____
3. _____

FOOD INTAKE

JOURNAL ENTRY/FREE SPACE...

DATE: _____ S M T W T F S   HOURS SLEPT: _____

MORNING MOOD

😀 🙂 😐 🙁 😞

ENERGY LEVEL

ACTIVITIES

♡ GOAL FOR TODAY...
♡♡ _____
♡♡♡ _____

❋ THREE THINGS I AM GRATEFUL FOR....

1. _____
2. _____
3. _____

FOOD INTAKE

JOURNAL ENTRY/FREE SPACE...

EVENING MOOD

😀 🙂 😐 🙁 😞

ENERGY LEVEL

ACTIVITIES

TODAY I WAS ANXIOUS ABOUT...
_____
_____

❋ THREE POSITIVE THINGS ABOUT MY DAY WERE:

1. _____
2. _____
3. _____

FOOD INTAKE

JOURNAL ENTRY/FREE SPACE...

DATE: _____ S M T W T F S   HOURS SLEPT: _____

MORNING MOOD
😃 🙂 😐 🙁 ☹️

ENERGY LEVEL

ACTIVITIES

GOAL FOR TODAY...
♡ _____
♡♡ _____
♡♡♡ _____

❊ THREE THINGS I AM GRATEFUL FOR....
1. _____
2. _____
3. _____

FOOD INTAKE

JOURNAL ENTRY/FREE SPACE...

· + ✳ · • ★ ✳ ○ ✱ ※ ✱ ○ ✳ ✶ • ✳ ✦ ·

EVENING MOOD
😃 🙂 😐 🙁 ☹️

ENERGY LEVEL

ACTIVITIES

TODAY I WAS ANXIOUS ABOUT...
_____
_____
_____

❊ THREE POSITIVE THINGS ABOUT MY DAY WERE:
1. _____
2. _____
3. _____

FOOD INTAKE

JOURNAL ENTRY/FREE SPACE...

DATE: _____ S M T W T F S   HOURS SLEPT: _____

MORNING MOOD

😊 🙂 😐 🙁 ☹️

ENERGY LEVEL

ACTIVITIES

♡ GOAL FOR TODAY... _____
♡♡ _____
♡♡♡ _____

❈ THREE THINGS I AM GRATEFUL FOR....

1. _____
2. _____
3. _____

FOOD INTAKE

JOURNAL ENTRY/FREE SPACE...

EVENING MOOD

😊 🙂 😐 🙁 ☹️

ENERGY LEVEL

ACTIVITIES

TODAY I WAS ANXIOUS ABOUT...
_____
_____
_____

❈ THREE POSITIVE THINGS ABOUT MY DAY WERE:

1. _____
2. _____
3. _____

FOOD INTAKE

JOURNAL ENTRY/FREE SPACE...

DATE: _____ S M T W T F S   HOURS SLEPT: _____

MORNING MOOD
😀 🙂 😐 🙁 😠

ENERGY LEVEL

ACTIVITIES

GOAL FOR TODAY...
♡ _____
♡♡ _____
♡♡♡ _____

❋ THREE THINGS I AM GRATEFUL FOR....
1. _____
2. _____
3. _____

FOOD INTAKE

JOURNAL ENTRY/FREE SPACE...

· + ❋ · * ❋ o ❋ ☀ ❋ o ❋ * · ❋ + ·

EVENING MOOD
😀 🙂 😐 🙁 😠

ENERGY LEVEL

ACTIVITIES

TODAY I WAS ANXIOUS ABOUT...
_____
_____

❋ THREE POSITIVE THINGS ABOUT MY DAY WERE:
1. _____
2. _____
3. _____

FOOD INTAKE

JOURNAL ENTRY/FREE SPACE...

DATE: _____ S M T W T F S   HOURS SLEPT: _____

MORNING MOOD
😊 🙂 😐 🙁 ☹️

ENERGY LEVEL
_____
_____
_____

ACTIVITIES

♡ GOAL FOR TODAY...
_____
♡♡ _____
♡♡♡ _____

❊ THREE THINGS I AM GRATEFUL FOR....
1. _____
2. _____
3. _____

FOOD INTAKE
_____
_____
_____
_____

JOURNAL ENTRY/FREE SPACE...

· + ❋ · ✱ ❋ · ○ ❋ ☼ ✳ ○ ❋ ✱ · ❋ ✢ ·

EVENING MOOD
😊 🙂 😐 🙁 ☹️

ENERGY LEVEL
_____
_____
_____

ACTIVITIES

TODAY I WAS ANXIOUS ABOUT...
_____
_____
_____

❊ THREE POSITIVE THINGS ABOUT MY DAY WERE:
1. _____
2. _____
3. _____

FOOD INTAKE
_____
_____
_____
_____

JOURNAL ENTRY/FREE SPACE...

DATE: _____ S M T W T F S   HOURS SLEPT: _____

MORNING MOOD
😃 🙂 😐 🙁 😣

ENERGY LEVEL
_____
_____
_____

ACTIVITIES

GOAL FOR TODAY...
♡ _____
♡♡ _____
♡♡♡ _____

❀ THREE THINGS I AM GRATEFUL FOR....
1. _____
2. _____
3. _____

FOOD INTAKE
_____
_____
_____
_____

JOURNAL ENTRY/FREE SPACE...

· + ✶ • ✱ ✳ ○ ✻ ☀ ✶ ○ ✱ ✦ • ✶ ✢ ·

EVENING MOOD
😃 🙂 😐 🙁 😣

ENERGY LEVEL
_____
_____
_____

ACTIVITIES

TODAY I WAS ANXIOUS ABOUT...
_____
_____
_____

❀ THREE POSITIVE THINGS ABOUT MY DAY WERE:
1. _____
2. _____
3. _____

FOOD INTAKE
_____
_____
_____
_____

JOURNAL ENTRY/FREE SPACE...

DATE: _____ S M T W T F S   HOURS SLEPT: _____

MORNING MOOD

☺ ☺ 😐 ☹ 😖

ENERGY LEVEL
_____
_____
_____

ACTIVITIES

♡ GOAL FOR TODAY... _____
♡♡ _____
♡♡♡ _____

❁ THREE THINGS I AM GRATEFUL FOR....

1. _____
2. _____
3. _____

FOOD INTAKE
_____
_____
_____
_____

JOURNAL ENTRY/FREE SPACE...

· + ✱ · ✦ ✱ ○ ✱ ⚡ ✱ ○ ✱ ✦ · ✱ + ·

EVENING MOOD

☺ ☺ 😐 ☹ 😖

ENERGY LEVEL
_____
_____
_____

ACTIVITIES

TODAY I WAS ANXIOUS ABOUT...
_____
_____
_____

❁ THREE POSITIVE THINGS ABOUT MY DAY WERE:

1. _____
2. _____
3. _____

FOOD INTAKE
_____
_____
_____
_____

JOURNAL ENTRY/FREE SPACE...

DATE: ———————— S M T W T F S   HOURS SLEPT: ————————

MORNING MOOD
😊 🙂 😐 🙁 😣

ENERGY LEVEL

ACTIVITIES

GOAL FOR TODAY...
♡ ————————————————————
♡♡ ————————————————————
♡♡♡ ————————————————————

❀ THREE THINGS I AM GRATEFUL FOR....
1. ————————————————————————
2. ————————————————————————
3. ————————————————————————

FOOD INTAKE

JOURNAL ENTRY/FREE SPACE...

· + ✻ · ✱ ✻ o ✵ ☀ ✱ o ✶ ✱ · ✻ + ·

EVENING MOOD
😊 🙂 😐 🙁 😣

ENERGY LEVEL

ACTIVITIES

TODAY I WAS ANXIOUS ABOUT...
————————————————————————
————————————————————————

❀ THREE POSITIVE THINGS ABOUT MY DAY WERE:
1. ————————————————————————
2. ————————————————————————
3. ————————————————————————

FOOD INTAKE

JOURNAL ENTRY/FREE SPACE...

DATE: _____ S M T W T F S   HOURS SLEPT: _____

MORNING MOOD

☺ ☺ 😐 ☹ ☹

ENERGY LEVEL
_____
_____
_____

ACTIVITIES

♡ GOAL FOR TODAY... _____
♡♡ _____
♡♡♡ _____

❁ THREE THINGS I AM GRATEFUL FOR....

1. _____
2. _____
3. _____

FOOD INTAKE
_____
_____
_____

JOURNAL ENTRY/FREE SPACE...

EVENING MOOD

☺ ☺ 😐 ☹ ☹

ENERGY LEVEL
_____
_____
_____

ACTIVITIES

TODAY I WAS ANXIOUS ABOUT...
_____
_____
_____

❁ THREE POSITIVE THINGS ABOUT MY DAY WERE:

1. _____
2. _____
3. _____

FOOD INTAKE
_____
_____
_____

JOURNAL ENTRY/FREE SPACE...

DATE: _____ S M T W T F S   HOURS SLEPT: _____

MORNING MOOD
😀 😊 😐 🙁 ☹️

ENERGY LEVEL
_____
_____
_____

ACTIVITIES

GOAL FOR TODAY...
♡ _____
♡♡ _____
♡♡♡ _____

❀ THREE THINGS I AM GRATEFUL FOR....
1. _____
2. _____
3. _____

FOOD INTAKE
_____
_____
_____

JOURNAL ENTRY/FREE SPACE...

· + ✸ · ✱ ✻ ○ ✶ ☀ ✵ ○ ✴ ✦ · ✱ ✚ ·

EVENING MOOD
😀 😊 😐 🙁 ☹️

ENERGY LEVEL
_____
_____
_____

ACTIVITIES

TODAY I WAS ANXIOUS ABOUT...
_____
_____
_____

❀ THREE POSITIVE THINGS ABOUT MY DAY WERE:
1. _____
2. _____
3. _____

FOOD INTAKE
_____
_____
_____
_____

JOURNAL ENTRY/FREE SPACE...

DATE: _____ S M T W T F S   HOURS SLEPT: _____

MORNING MOOD
😊 🙂 😐 🙁 ☹️

ENERGY LEVEL
_____
_____
_____

ACTIVITIES

GOAL FOR TODAY...
♡ _____
♡♡ _____
♡♡♡ _____

❋ THREE THINGS I AM GRATEFUL FOR....
1. _____
2. _____
3. _____

FOOD INTAKE
_____
_____
_____

JOURNAL ENTRY/FREE SPACE...

· ✦ ✳ · ✳ ○ ✻ ✺ ✷ ○ ✶ ✱ · ✳ ✦ ·

EVENING MOOD
😊 🙂 😐 🙁 ☹️

ENERGY LEVEL
_____
_____
_____

ACTIVITIES

TODAY I WAS ANXIOUS ABOUT...
_____
_____

❋ THREE POSITIVE THINGS ABOUT MY DAY WERE:
1. _____
2. _____
3. _____

FOOD INTAKE
_____
_____
_____

JOURNAL ENTRY/FREE SPACE...

DATE: _____ S M T W T F S   HOURS SLEPT: _____

MORNING MOOD

☺ ☺ 😐 ☹ ☹

ENERGY LEVEL
_____
_____
_____

ACTIVITIES

GOAL FOR TODAY...
♡ _____
♡♡ _____
♡♡♡ _____

❀ THREE THINGS I AM GRATEFUL FOR....
1. _____
2. _____
3. _____

FOOD INTAKE
_____
_____
_____

JOURNAL ENTRY/FREE SPACE...

· ✢ ✱ · ★ ✱ ○ ✱ ☼ ✱ ○ ✱ ★ · ✱ ✢ ·

EVENING MOOD

☺ ☺ 😐 ☹ ☹

ENERGY LEVEL
_____
_____
_____

ACTIVITIES

TODAY I WAS ANXIOUS ABOUT...
_____
_____
_____

❀ THREE POSITIVE THINGS ABOUT MY DAY WERE:
1. _____
2. _____
3. _____

FOOD INTAKE
_____
_____
_____
_____

JOURNAL ENTRY/FREE SPACE...

DATE: ——————— S M T W T F S   HOURS SLEPT: ———————

MORNING MOOD
😊 🙂 😐 🙁 😟

ENERGY LEVEL
_____
_____
_____

ACTIVITIES

♡ GOAL FOR TODAY... _____
♡♡ _____
♡♡♡ _____

❊ THREE THINGS I AM GRATEFUL FOR....
1. _____
2. _____
3. _____

FOOD INTAKE
_____
_____
_____

JOURNAL ENTRY/FREE SPACE...

· + ✳ • ✦ ✱ ✶ ○ ❋ ✺ ✳ ○ ✱ ✦ • ✶ + ·

EVENING MOOD
😊 🙂 😐 🙁 😟

ENERGY LEVEL
_____
_____
_____

ACTIVITIES

TODAY I WAS ANXIOUS ABOUT...
_____
_____
_____

❊ THREE POSITIVE THINGS ABOUT MY DAY WERE:
1. _____
2. _____
3. _____

FOOD INTAKE
_____
_____
_____
_____

JOURNAL ENTRY/FREE SPACE...

DATE: _____ S M T W T F S   HOURS SLEPT: _____

MORNING MOOD

😀 🙂 😐 🙁 ☹️

ENERGY LEVEL
_____
_____
_____

ACTIVITIES

♡ GOAL FOR TODAY... _____
♡♡ _____
♡♡♡ _____

❀ THREE THINGS I AM GRATEFUL FOR....
1. _____
2. _____
3. _____

FOOD INTAKE
_____
_____
_____
_____

JOURNAL ENTRY/FREE SPACE...

· + ✶ • ✵ ✶ ○ ✳ ☀ ✱ ○ ✶ ✦ • ✶ + ·

EVENING MOOD

🙂 🙂 😐 🙁 ☹️

ENERGY LEVEL
_____
_____
_____

ACTIVITIES

TODAY I WAS ANXIOUS ABOUT...
_____
_____
_____

❀ THREE POSITIVE THINGS ABOUT MY DAY WERE:
1. _____
2. _____
3. _____

FOOD INTAKE
_____
_____
_____
_____

JOURNAL ENTRY/FREE SPACE...

DATE: _____ S M T W T F S   HOURS SLEPT: _____

MORNING MOOD

☺ ☺ 😐 ☹ ☹

ENERGY LEVEL

ACTIVITIES

♡ GOAL FOR TODAY...
♡♡ _____
♡♡♡ _____

❋ THREE THINGS I AM GRATEFUL FOR....

1. _____
2. _____
3. _____

FOOD INTAKE

JOURNAL ENTRY/FREE SPACE...

EVENING MOOD

☺ ☺ 😐 ☹ ☹

ENERGY LEVEL

ACTIVITIES

TODAY I WAS ANXIOUS ABOUT...
_____
_____
_____

❋ THREE POSITIVE THINGS ABOUT MY DAY WERE:

1. _____
2. _____
3. _____

FOOD INTAKE

JOURNAL ENTRY/FREE SPACE...

DATE: _____ S M T W T F S   HOURS SLEPT: _____

MORNING MOOD

😀 🙂 😐 🙁 ☹️

ENERGY LEVEL

ACTIVITIES

♡ GOAL FOR TODAY... _____
♡♡ _____
♡♡♡ _____

❋ THREE THINGS I AM GRATEFUL FOR....
1. _____
2. _____
3. _____

FOOD INTAKE
_____
_____
_____

JOURNAL ENTRY/FREE SPACE...

· + ❋ · ☆ ❋ · ❋ ☀ ❋ ○ ❋ ❋ · ❋ + ·

EVENING MOOD

😀 🙂 😐 🙁 ☹️

ENERGY LEVEL

ACTIVITIES

TODAY I WAS ANXIOUS ABOUT...
_____
_____

❋ THREE POSITIVE THINGS ABOUT MY DAY WERE:
1. _____
2. _____
3. _____

FOOD INTAKE
_____
_____
_____

JOURNAL ENTRY/FREE SPACE...

DATE: _____ S M T W T F S   HOURS SLEPT: _____

MORNING MOOD

😊 😊 😐 🙁 ☹️

ENERGY LEVEL

ACTIVITIES

♡ GOAL FOR TODAY... _____
♡♡ _____
♡♡♡ _____

❁ THREE THINGS I AM GRATEFUL FOR....

1. _____
2. _____
3. _____

FOOD INTAKE

_____
_____
_____

JOURNAL ENTRY/FREE SPACE...

· + ✻ · ✻ ✶ ◦ ✶ ☀ ✱ ◦ ✱ ✦ · ✻ + ·

EVENING MOOD

😊 😊 😐 🙁 ☹️

ENERGY LEVEL

ACTIVITIES

TODAY I WAS ANXIOUS ABOUT...
_____
_____
_____

❁ THREE POSITIVE THINGS ABOUT MY DAY WERE:

1. _____
2. _____
3. _____

FOOD INTAKE

_____
_____
_____

JOURNAL ENTRY/FREE SPACE...

DATE: _____ S M T W T F S   HOURS SLEPT: _____

MORNING MOOD

😀 🙂 😐 🙁 😟

ENERGY LEVEL
_____
_____
_____

ACTIVITIES

GOAL FOR TODAY...
♡ _____
♡♡ _____
♡♡♡ _____

❋ THREE THINGS I AM GRATEFUL FOR....

1. _____
2. _____
3. _____

FOOD INTAKE
_____
_____
_____

JOURNAL ENTRY/FREE SPACE...

EVENING MOOD

😀 🙂 😐 🙁 😟

ENERGY LEVEL
_____
_____
_____

ACTIVITIES

TODAY I WAS ANXIOUS ABOUT...
_____
_____
_____

❋ THREE POSITIVE THINGS ABOUT MY DAY WERE:

1. _____
2. _____
3. _____

FOOD INTAKE
_____
_____
_____

JOURNAL ENTRY/FREE SPACE...

DATE: _____ S M T W T F S   HOURS SLEPT: _____

MORNING MOOD
☺ ☺ 😐 ☹ ☹

ENERGY LEVEL

ACTIVITIES

GOAL FOR TODAY...
♡ _____
♡♡ _____
♡♡♡ _____

❋ THREE THINGS I AM GRATEFUL FOR....
1. _____
2. _____
3. _____

FOOD INTAKE

JOURNAL ENTRY/FREE SPACE...

EVENING MOOD
☺ ☺ 😐 ☹ ☹

ENERGY LEVEL

ACTIVITIES

TODAY I WAS ANXIOUS ABOUT...
_____
_____

❋ THREE POSITIVE THINGS ABOUT MY DAY WERE:
1. _____
2. _____
3. _____

FOOD INTAKE

JOURNAL ENTRY/FREE SPACE...

DATE: _____ S M T W T F S   HOURS SLEPT: _____

MORNING MOOD

☺ ☺ 😐 ☹ 😟

ENERGY LEVEL
_____
_____
_____

ACTIVITIES

♡ GOAL FOR TODAY...
_____
♡♡ _____
♡♡♡ _____

❋ THREE THINGS I AM GRATEFUL FOR....

1. _____
2. _____
3. _____

FOOD INTAKE
_____
_____
_____

JOURNAL ENTRY/FREE SPACE...

· + ✱ · ★ ✳ o ✲ ☀ ✱ o ✳ ★ · ✳ ✢ ·

EVENING MOOD

☺ ☺ 😐 ☹ 😟

ENERGY LEVEL
_____
_____
_____

ACTIVITIES

TODAY I WAS ANXIOUS ABOUT...
_____
_____

❋ THREE POSITIVE THINGS ABOUT MY DAY WERE:

1. _____
2. _____
3. _____

FOOD INTAKE
_____
_____
_____

JOURNAL ENTRY/FREE SPACE...

DATE: _____ S M T W T F S   HOURS SLEPT: _____

MORNING MOOD
😊 😊 😐 🙁 ☹️

ENERGY LEVEL
_____
_____
_____

ACTIVITIES

♡ GOAL FOR TODAY... _____
♡♡ _____
♡♡♡ _____

❃ THREE THINGS I AM GRATEFUL FOR....
1. _____
2. _____
3. _____

FOOD INTAKE
_____
_____
_____

JOURNAL ENTRY/FREE SPACE...

· + ❋ • ✷ ❋ o ❋ ☀ ✶ o ❋ ★ • ❋ + ·

EVENING MOOD
😊 😊 😐 🙁 ☹️

ENERGY LEVEL
_____
_____
_____

ACTIVITIES

TODAY I WAS ANXIOUS ABOUT...
_____
_____
_____

❃ THREE POSITIVE THINGS ABOUT MY DAY WERE:
1. _____
2. _____
3. _____

FOOD INTAKE
_____
_____
_____

JOURNAL ENTRY/FREE SPACE...

DATE: _____ S M T W T F S   HOURS SLEPT: _____

MORNING MOOD

😊 🙂 😐 🙁 ☹️

ENERGY LEVEL

ACTIVITIES

♡ GOAL FOR TODAY...
♡♡ _____
♡♡♡ _____

❀ THREE THINGS I AM GRATEFUL FOR....
1.
2.
3.

FOOD INTAKE

JOURNAL ENTRY/FREE SPACE...

EVENING MOOD

😊 🙂 😐 🙁 ☹️

ENERGY LEVEL

ACTIVITIES

TODAY I WAS ANXIOUS ABOUT...

❀ THREE POSITIVE THINGS ABOUT MY DAY WERE:
1.
2.
3.

FOOD INTAKE

JOURNAL ENTRY/FREE SPACE...

DATE: _____ S M T W T F S   HOURS SLEPT: _____

MORNING MOOD

ENERGY LEVEL

ACTIVITIES

GOAL FOR TODAY...
♡ _____
♡♡ _____
♡♡♡ _____

❋ THREE THINGS I AM GRATEFUL FOR....
1. _____
2. _____
3. _____

FOOD INTAKE

JOURNAL ENTRY/FREE SPACE...

· + ❋ · ❋ ❋ ○ ❋ ☀ ❋ ○ ❋ ❋ · ❋ + ·

EVENING MOOD

ENERGY LEVEL

ACTIVITIES

TODAY I WAS ANXIOUS ABOUT...
_____
_____
_____

❋ THREE POSITIVE THINGS ABOUT MY DAY WERE:
1. _____
2. _____
3. _____

FOOD INTAKE

JOURNAL ENTRY/FREE SPACE...

DATE: _____ S M T W T F S   HOURS SLEPT: _____

MORNING MOOD

😀 🙂 😐 🙁 😟

ENERGY LEVEL
_____
_____
_____

ACTIVITIES

GOAL FOR TODAY...
♡ _____
♡♡ _____
♡♡♡ _____

❀ THREE THINGS I AM GRATEFUL FOR....
1. _____
2. _____
3. _____

FOOD INTAKE
_____
_____
_____

JOURNAL ENTRY/FREE SPACE...

EVENING MOOD

😀 🙂 😐 🙁 😟

ENERGY LEVEL
_____
_____
_____

ACTIVITIES

TODAY I WAS ANXIOUS ABOUT...
_____
_____

❀ THREE POSITIVE THINGS ABOUT MY DAY WERE:
1. _____
2. _____
3. _____

FOOD INTAKE
_____
_____
_____

JOURNAL ENTRY/FREE SPACE...

DATE: _____ S M T W T F S   HOURS SLEPT: _____

MORNING MOOD
😊 🙂 😐 🙁 😣

ENERGY LEVEL
_____
_____
_____

ACTIVITIES

GOAL FOR TODAY...
♡ _____
♡♡ _____
♡♡♡ _____

❀ THREE THINGS I AM GRATEFUL FOR....
1. _____
2. _____
3. _____

FOOD INTAKE
_____
_____
_____

JOURNAL ENTRY/FREE SPACE...

· ✴ * · * * ✺ ✳ ○ ✱ * · ✱ + ·

EVENING MOOD
😊 🙂 😐 🙁 😣

ENERGY LEVEL
_____
_____
_____

ACTIVITIES

TODAY I WAS ANXIOUS ABOUT...
_____
_____
_____

❀ THREE POSITIVE THINGS ABOUT MY DAY WERE:
1. _____
2. _____
3. _____

FOOD INTAKE
_____
_____
_____

JOURNAL ENTRY/FREE SPACE...

DATE: _____ S M T W T F S   HOURS SLEPT: _____

MORNING MOOD

😀 🙂 😐 🙁 😣

ENERGY LEVEL
_____
_____
_____

ACTIVITIES

GOAL FOR TODAY...
♡ _____
♡♡ _____
♡♡♡ _____

❀ THREE THINGS I AM GRATEFUL FOR....
1. _____
2. _____
3. _____

FOOD INTAKE
_____
_____
_____

JOURNAL ENTRY/FREE SPACE...

EVENING MOOD

😀 🙂 😐 🙁 😣

ENERGY LEVEL
_____
_____
_____

ACTIVITIES

TODAY I WAS ANXIOUS ABOUT...
_____
_____
_____

❀ THREE POSITIVE THINGS ABOUT MY DAY WERE:
1. _____
2. _____
3. _____

FOOD INTAKE
_____
_____
_____
_____

JOURNAL ENTRY/FREE SPACE...

DATE: _____ S M T W T F S   HOURS SLEPT: _____

MORNING MOOD

☺ ☺ 😐 ☹ ☹

ENERGY LEVEL

ACTIVITIES

GOAL FOR TODAY...
♡ _____
♡♡ _____
♡♡♡ _____

❋ THREE THINGS I AM GRATEFUL FOR....
1. _____
2. _____
3. _____

FOOD INTAKE

JOURNAL ENTRY/FREE SPACE...

EVENING MOOD

☺ ☺ 😐 ☹ ☹

ENERGY LEVEL

ACTIVITIES

TODAY I WAS ANXIOUS ABOUT...
_____
_____
_____

❋ THREE POSITIVE THINGS ABOUT MY DAY WERE:
1. _____
2. _____
3. _____

FOOD INTAKE

JOURNAL ENTRY/FREE SPACE...

DATE: _____ S M T W T F S   HOURS SLEPT: _____

MORNING MOOD
😊 🙂 😐 🙁 ☹️

ENERGY LEVEL
_____
_____
_____

ACTIVITIES

GOAL FOR TODAY...
♡ _____
♡♡ _____
♡♡♡ _____

❁ THREE THINGS I AM GRATEFUL FOR....
1. _____
2. _____
3. _____

FOOD INTAKE
_____
_____
_____

JOURNAL ENTRY/FREE SPACE...

EVENING MOOD
😊 🙂 😐 🙁 ☹️

ENERGY LEVEL
_____
_____
_____

ACTIVITIES

TODAY I WAS ANXIOUS ABOUT...
_____
_____
_____

❁ THREE POSITIVE THINGS ABOUT MY DAY WERE:
1. _____
2. _____
3. _____

FOOD INTAKE
_____
_____
_____

JOURNAL ENTRY/FREE SPACE...

DATE: _____ S M T W T F S   HOURS SLEPT: _____

MORNING MOOD

ENERGY LEVEL

ACTIVITIES

♡ GOAL FOR TODAY... _____
♡♡ _____
♡♡♡ _____

❋ THREE THINGS I AM GRATEFUL FOR....
1. _____
2. _____
3. _____

FOOD INTAKE

JOURNAL ENTRY/FREE SPACE...

EVENING MOOD

ENERGY LEVEL

ACTIVITIES

TODAY I WAS ANXIOUS ABOUT...
_____
_____

❋ THREE POSITIVE THINGS ABOUT MY DAY WERE:
1. _____
2. _____
3. _____

FOOD INTAKE

JOURNAL ENTRY/FREE SPACE...

DATE: _____ S M T W T F S   HOURS SLEPT: _____

MORNING MOOD

😃 🙂 😐 🙁 😟

ENERGY LEVEL

ACTIVITIES

GOAL FOR TODAY...
♡ _____
♡♡ _____
♡♡♡ _____

❋ THREE THINGS I AM GRATEFUL FOR....
1. _____
2. _____
3. _____

FOOD INTAKE

JOURNAL ENTRY/FREE SPACE...

· ✦ ✶ · ✳ ✷ ○ ✺ ✦ ✱ ○ ✳ ✶ · ✷ ✦ ·

EVENING MOOD

😃 🙂 😐 🙁 😟

ENERGY LEVEL

ACTIVITIES

TODAY I WAS ANXIOUS ABOUT...
_____
_____
_____

❋ THREE POSITIVE THINGS ABOUT MY DAY WERE:
1. _____
2. _____
3. _____

FOOD INTAKE

JOURNAL ENTRY/FREE SPACE...

DATE: _____ S M T W T F S   HOURS SLEPT: _____

MORNING MOOD

☺ ☺ 😐 ☹ ☹

ENERGY LEVEL
_____
_____
_____

ACTIVITIES

♡ GOAL FOR TODAY...
♡♡ _____
♡♡♡ _____

✿ THREE THINGS I AM GRATEFUL FOR....
1. _____
2. _____
3. _____

FOOD INTAKE
_____
_____
_____

JOURNAL ENTRY/FREE SPACE...

· + ✦ · ✳ · ✦ ○ ✷ ☀ ✶ ○ ✳ ★ · ✦ + ·

EVENING MOOD

☺ ☺ 😐 ☹ ☹

ENERGY LEVEL
_____
_____
_____

ACTIVITIES

TODAY I WAS ANXIOUS ABOUT...
_____
_____

✿ THREE POSITIVE THINGS ABOUT MY DAY WERE:
1. _____
2. _____
3. _____

FOOD INTAKE
_____
_____
_____

JOURNAL ENTRY/FREE SPACE...

DATE: _____ S M T W T F S   HOURS SLEPT: _____

MORNING MOOD

☺ ☺ 😐 ☹ ☹

ENERGY LEVEL
_____
_____
_____

ACTIVITIES

♡ GOAL FOR TODAY...
♡♡ _____
♡♡♡ _____

❀ THREE THINGS I AM GRATEFUL FOR....

1. _____
2. _____
3. _____

FOOD INTAKE
_____
_____
_____

JOURNAL ENTRY/FREE SPACE...

· + ✽ · ✳ ✻ o ✱ ☀ ✶ o ✳ ✦ · ✽ + ·

EVENING MOOD

☺ ☺ 😐 ☹ ☹

ENERGY LEVEL
_____
_____
_____

ACTIVITIES

TODAY I WAS ANXIOUS ABOUT...
_____
_____

❀ THREE POSITIVE THINGS ABOUT MY DAY WERE:

1. _____
2. _____
3. _____

FOOD INTAKE
_____
_____
_____

JOURNAL ENTRY/FREE SPACE...

DATE: _____ S M T W T F S   HOURS SLEPT: _____

MORNING MOOD
☺ ☺ 😐 ☹ ☹

ENERGY LEVEL
_____
_____
_____

ACTIVITIES

♡ GOAL FOR TODAY... _____
♡♡ _____
♡♡♡ _____

❀ THREE THINGS I AM GRATEFUL FOR....
1. _____
2. _____
3. _____

FOOD INTAKE
_____
_____
_____
_____

JOURNAL ENTRY/FREE SPACE...

· + ✳ · ✱ ✳ ○ ✳ ☀ ✱ ○ ✳ ✦ · ✱ + ·

EVENING MOOD
☺ ☺ 😐 ☹ ☹

ENERGY LEVEL
_____
_____
_____

ACTIVITIES

TODAY I WAS ANXIOUS ABOUT...
_____
_____
_____

❀ THREE POSITIVE THINGS ABOUT MY DAY WERE:
1. _____
2. _____
3. _____

FOOD INTAKE
_____
_____
_____
_____

JOURNAL ENTRY/FREE SPACE...

DATE: _____ S M T W T F S   HOURS SLEPT: _____

MORNING MOOD

😊 🙂 😐 🙁 ☹

ENERGY LEVEL
_____
_____
_____

ACTIVITIES

GOAL FOR TODAY...
♡ _____
♡♡ _____
♡♡♡ _____

❊ THREE THINGS I AM GRATEFUL FOR....
1. _____
2. _____
3. _____

FOOD INTAKE
_____
_____
_____

JOURNAL ENTRY/FREE SPACE...

· ✢ ✻ · ✳ ✱ ○ ✱ ✺ ✶ ○ ✳ ✱ · ✱ ✢ ·

EVENING MOOD

😊 🙂 😐 🙁 ☹

ENERGY LEVEL
_____
_____
_____

ACTIVITIES

TODAY I WAS ANXIOUS ABOUT...
_____
_____

❊ THREE POSITIVE THINGS ABOUT MY DAY WERE:
1. _____
2. _____
3. _____

FOOD INTAKE
_____
_____
_____

JOURNAL ENTRY/FREE SPACE...

DATE: _____ S M T W T F S   HOURS SLEPT: _____

MORNING MOOD

😊 😃 😐 ☹️ 😢

ENERGY LEVEL

ACTIVITIES

♡ GOAL FOR TODAY... _____
♡♡ _____
♡♡♡ _____

❊ THREE THINGS I AM GRATEFUL FOR....
1. _____
2. _____
3. _____

FOOD INTAKE

JOURNAL ENTRY/FREE SPACE...

· + ✱ · • ✱ ○ ✱ ☀ ✱ ○ ✱ ✱ • ✱ + ·

EVENING MOOD

😊 😃 😐 ☹️ 😢

ENERGY LEVEL

ACTIVITIES

TODAY I WAS ANXIOUS ABOUT...
_____
_____
_____

❊ THREE POSITIVE THINGS ABOUT MY DAY WERE:
1. _____
2. _____
3. _____

FOOD INTAKE

JOURNAL ENTRY/FREE SPACE...

DATE: _____ S M T W T F S   HOURS SLEPT: _____

MORNING MOOD

😊 🙂 😐 🙁 ☹️

ENERGY LEVEL
_____
_____
_____

ACTIVITIES

♡ GOAL FOR TODAY...
♡♡ _____
♡♡♡ _____

❀ THREE THINGS I AM GRATEFUL FOR....

1. _____
2. _____
3. _____

FOOD INTAKE
_____
_____
_____

JOURNAL ENTRY/FREE SPACE...

· + ✱ · • ✴ ○ ✶ ✺ ✳ ○ ✱ ✦ • ✶ ✢ ·

EVENING MOOD

😊 🙂 😐 🙁 ☹️

ENERGY LEVEL
_____
_____
_____

ACTIVITIES

TODAY I WAS ANXIOUS ABOUT...
_____
_____
_____

❀ THREE POSITIVE THINGS ABOUT MY DAY WERE:

1. _____
2. _____
3. _____

FOOD INTAKE
_____
_____
_____

JOURNAL ENTRY/FREE SPACE...

DATE: _____ S M T W T F S   HOURS SLEPT: _____

MORNING MOOD
☺ ☺ 😐 ☹ ☹

ENERGY LEVEL
_____
_____
_____

ACTIVITIES

♡ GOAL FOR TODAY... _____
♡♡ _____
♡♡♡ _____

❋ THREE THINGS I AM GRATEFUL FOR....
1. _____
2. _____
3. _____

FOOD INTAKE
_____
_____
_____
_____

JOURNAL ENTRY/FREE SPACE...

· ✦ ✱ · ✳ ✱ ○ ✱ ☀ ✱ ○ ✱ ✦ · ✱ ✦ ·

EVENING MOOD
☺ ☺ 😐 ☹ ☹

ENERGY LEVEL
_____
_____
_____

ACTIVITIES

TODAY I WAS ANXIOUS ABOUT...
_____
_____
_____

❋ THREE POSITIVE THINGS ABOUT MY DAY WERE:
1. _____
2. _____
3. _____

FOOD INTAKE
_____
_____
_____
_____

JOURNAL ENTRY/FREE SPACE...

DATE: _____ S M T W T F S   HOURS SLEPT: _____

MORNING MOOD

😊 🙂 😐 🙁 😟

ENERGY LEVEL
_____
_____
_____

ACTIVITIES

GOAL FOR TODAY...
♡ _____
♡♡ _____
♡♡♡ _____

❋ THREE THINGS I AM GRATEFUL FOR....

1. _____
2. _____
3. _____

FOOD INTAKE
_____
_____
_____
_____

JOURNAL ENTRY/FREE SPACE...

· + * · * ✱ ○ * ✺ * ○ * ★ · * + ·

EVENING MOOD

😊 🙂 😐 🙁 😟

ENERGY LEVEL
_____
_____
_____

ACTIVITIES

TODAY I WAS ANXIOUS ABOUT...
_____
_____
_____

❋ THREE POSITIVE THINGS ABOUT MY DAY WERE:

1. _____
2. _____
3. _____

FOOD INTAKE
_____
_____
_____
_____

JOURNAL ENTRY/FREE SPACE...

DATE: _____ S M T W T F S   HOURS SLEPT: _____

MORNING MOOD

☺ ☺ 😐 ☹ ☹

ENERGY LEVEL

ACTIVITIES

GOAL FOR TODAY...
♡ _____
♡♡ _____
♡♡♡ _____

❀ THREE THINGS I AM GRATEFUL FOR....

1. _____
2. _____
3. _____

FOOD INTAKE

JOURNAL ENTRY/FREE SPACE...

EVENING MOOD

☺ ☺ 😐 ☹ ☹

ENERGY LEVEL

ACTIVITIES

TODAY I WAS ANXIOUS ABOUT...
_____
_____

❀ THREE POSITIVE THINGS ABOUT MY DAY WERE:

1. _____
2. _____
3. _____

FOOD INTAKE

JOURNAL ENTRY/FREE SPACE...

DATE: _____ S M T W T F S   HOURS SLEPT: _____

MORNING MOOD

😊 🙂 😐 🙁 ☹️

ENERGY LEVEL

ACTIVITIES

GOAL FOR TODAY...
♡ _____
♡♡ _____
♡♡♡ _____

❀ THREE THINGS I AM GRATEFUL FOR....

1. _____
2. _____
3. _____

FOOD INTAKE

JOURNAL ENTRY/FREE SPACE...

EVENING MOOD

😊 🙂 😐 🙁 ☹️

ENERGY LEVEL

ACTIVITIES

TODAY I WAS ANXIOUS ABOUT...
_____
_____

❀ THREE POSITIVE THINGS ABOUT MY DAY WERE:

1. _____
2. _____
3. _____

FOOD INTAKE

JOURNAL ENTRY/FREE SPACE...

DATE: _____ S M T W T F S   HOURS SLEPT: _____

MORNING MOOD

☺ ☺ 😐 ☹ ☹

ENERGY LEVEL

ACTIVITIES

GOAL FOR TODAY...
♡ _____
♡♡ _____
♡♡♡ _____

❋ THREE THINGS I AM GRATEFUL FOR....

1. _____
2. _____
3. _____

FOOD INTAKE

JOURNAL ENTRY/FREE SPACE...

EVENING MOOD

☺ ☺ 😐 ☹ ☹

ENERGY LEVEL

ACTIVITIES

TODAY I WAS ANXIOUS ABOUT...
_____
_____
_____

❋ THREE POSITIVE THINGS ABOUT MY DAY WERE:

1. _____
2. _____
3. _____

FOOD INTAKE

JOURNAL ENTRY/FREE SPACE...

DATE: _____ S M T W T F S   HOURS SLEPT: _____

MORNING MOOD

😀 🙂 😐 🙁 😣

ENERGY LEVEL
_____
_____
_____

ACTIVITIES

GOAL FOR TODAY...
♡ _____
♡♡ _____
♡♡♡ _____

❋ THREE THINGS I AM GRATEFUL FOR....

1. _____
2. _____
3. _____

FOOD INTAKE
_____
_____
_____
_____

JOURNAL ENTRY/FREE SPACE...

· ✦ ✱ · ✹ ✱ o ✱ ✺ ✱ o ✱ ✦ · ✱ ✦ ·

EVENING MOOD

😀 🙂 😐 🙁 😣

ENERGY LEVEL
_____
_____
_____

ACTIVITIES

TODAY I WAS ANXIOUS ABOUT...
_____
_____
_____

❋ THREE POSITIVE THINGS ABOUT MY DAY WERE:

1. _____
2. _____
3. _____

FOOD INTAKE
_____
_____
_____
_____

JOURNAL ENTRY/FREE SPACE...

DATE: _____ S M T W T F S   HOURS SLEPT: _____

MORNING MOOD

😊 🙂 😐 🙁 ☹️

ENERGY LEVEL

ACTIVITIES

GOAL FOR TODAY...
♡ _____
♡♡ _____
♡♡♡ _____

❋ THREE THINGS I AM GRATEFUL FOR....

1. _____
2. _____
3. _____

FOOD INTAKE

JOURNAL ENTRY/FREE SPACE...

· + ✳ · ★ ✳ ○ ✶ ☀ ✱ ○ ✳ ★ · ✳ + ·

EVENING MOOD

😊 🙂 😐 🙁 ☹️

ENERGY LEVEL

ACTIVITIES

TODAY I WAS ANXIOUS ABOUT...
_____
_____
_____

❋ THREE POSITIVE THINGS ABOUT MY DAY WERE:

1. _____
2. _____
3. _____

FOOD INTAKE

JOURNAL ENTRY/FREE SPACE...

DATE: _____ S M T W T F S   HOURS SLEPT: _____

MORNING MOOD
😀 🙂 😐 🙁 😣

ENERGY LEVEL
_____
_____
_____

ACTIVITIES

GOAL FOR TODAY...
♡ _____
♡♡ _____
♡♡♡ _____

❀ THREE THINGS I AM GRATEFUL FOR....
1. _____
2. _____
3. _____

FOOD INTAKE
_____
_____
_____
_____

JOURNAL ENTRY/FREE SPACE...

· + ❋ · ✦ ❋ ○ ❋ ☀ ✱ ○ ❋ ✦ · ❋ + ·

EVENING MOOD
😀 🙂 😐 🙁 😣

ENERGY LEVEL
_____
_____
_____

ACTIVITIES

TODAY I WAS ANXIOUS ABOUT...
_____
_____
_____

❀ THREE POSITIVE THINGS ABOUT MY DAY WERE:
1. _____
2. _____
3. _____

FOOD INTAKE
_____
_____
_____
_____

JOURNAL ENTRY/FREE SPACE...

DATE: _____ S M T W T F S   HOURS SLEPT: _____

MORNING MOOD

😀 🙂 😐 🙁 😣

ENERGY LEVEL

ACTIVITIES

♡ GOAL FOR TODAY...
♡♡ _____
♡♡♡ _____

❀ THREE THINGS I AM GRATEFUL FOR....

1. _____
2. _____
3. _____

FOOD INTAKE

JOURNAL ENTRY/FREE SPACE...

EVENING MOOD

😀 🙂 😐 🙁 😣

ENERGY LEVEL

ACTIVITIES

TODAY I WAS ANXIOUS ABOUT...
_____
_____

❀ THREE POSITIVE THINGS ABOUT MY DAY WERE:

1. _____
2. _____
3. _____

FOOD INTAKE

JOURNAL ENTRY/FREE SPACE...

DATE: _____ S M T W T F S   HOURS SLEPT: _____

MORNING MOOD
😊 🙂 😐 🙁 😟

ENERGY LEVEL
_____
_____
_____

ACTIVITIES

GOAL FOR TODAY...
♡ _____
♡♡ _____
♡♡♡ _____

❀ THREE THINGS I AM GRATEFUL FOR....
1. _____
2. _____
3. _____

FOOD INTAKE
_____
_____
_____
_____

JOURNAL ENTRY/FREE SPACE...

· + ✳ · ✳ ✳ ○ ✳ ☀ ✳ ○ ✳ ★ · ✳ + ·

EVENING MOOD
😊 🙂 😐 🙁 😟

ENERGY LEVEL
_____
_____
_____

ACTIVITIES

TODAY I WAS ANXIOUS ABOUT...
_____
_____
_____

❀ THREE POSITIVE THINGS ABOUT MY DAY WERE:
1. _____
2. _____
3. _____

FOOD INTAKE
_____
_____
_____
_____

JOURNAL ENTRY/FREE SPACE...

DATE: _____ S M T W T F S   HOURS SLEPT: _____

MORNING MOOD

😊 😀 😐 🙁 ☹️

ENERGY LEVEL
_____
_____
_____

ACTIVITIES

♡ GOAL FOR TODAY...
_____
♡♡ _____
♡♡♡ _____

❀ THREE THINGS I AM GRATEFUL FOR....
1. _____
2. _____
3. _____

FOOD INTAKE
_____
_____
_____

JOURNAL ENTRY/FREE SPACE...

· + ✴ · ✳ ✺ o ✳ 🌟 ✶ o ✷ ★ · ✴ ✢ ·

EVENING MOOD

😊 😀 😐 🙁 ☹️

ENERGY LEVEL
_____
_____
_____

ACTIVITIES

TODAY I WAS ANXIOUS ABOUT...
_____
_____
_____

❀ THREE POSITIVE THINGS ABOUT MY DAY WERE:
1. _____
2. _____
3. _____

FOOD INTAKE
_____
_____
_____
_____

JOURNAL ENTRY/FREE SPACE...

DATE: _____ S M T W T F S   HOURS SLEPT: _____

MORNING MOOD

😊 🙂 😐 🙁 ☹

ENERGY LEVEL
_____
_____
_____

ACTIVITIES

GOAL FOR TODAY...
♡ _____
♡♡ _____
♡♡♡ _____

❋ THREE THINGS I AM GRATEFUL FOR....

1. _____
2. _____
3. _____

FOOD INTAKE
_____
_____
_____
_____

JOURNAL ENTRY/FREE SPACE...

· ✦ ✱ · ✱ ✱ ○ ✱ ☀ ✱ ○ ✱ ✱ · ✱ ✦ ·

EVENING MOOD

😊 🙂 😐 🙁 ☹

ENERGY LEVEL
_____
_____
_____

ACTIVITIES

TODAY I WAS ANXIOUS ABOUT...
_____
_____

❋ THREE POSITIVE THINGS ABOUT MY DAY WERE:

1. _____
2. _____
3. _____

FOOD INTAKE
_____
_____
_____
_____

JOURNAL ENTRY/FREE SPACE...

DATE: _____ S M T W T F S   HOURS SLEPT: _____

MORNING MOOD

ENERGY LEVEL

ACTIVITIES

GOAL FOR TODAY...
♡ _____
♡♡ _____
♡♡♡ _____

❃ THREE THINGS I AM GRATEFUL FOR....
1. _____
2. _____
3. _____

FOOD INTAKE

JOURNAL ENTRY/FREE SPACE...

EVENING MOOD

ENERGY LEVEL

ACTIVITIES

TODAY I WAS ANXIOUS ABOUT...
_____
_____

❃ THREE POSITIVE THINGS ABOUT MY DAY WERE:
1. _____
2. _____
3. _____

FOOD INTAKE

JOURNAL ENTRY/FREE SPACE...

DATE: _____ S M T W T F S   HOURS SLEPT: _____

MORNING MOOD

☺ ☺ 😐 ☹ 😖

ENERGY LEVEL

ACTIVITIES

GOAL FOR TODAY...
♡ _____
♡♡ _____
♡♡♡ _____

❀ THREE THINGS I AM GRATEFUL FOR....

1. _____
2. _____
3. _____

FOOD INTAKE

JOURNAL ENTRY/FREE SPACE...

. + ✻ • ✦ ✹ o ✶ ☀ ✗ o ✳ ✱ • ✳ ✦ ·

EVENING MOOD

☺ ☺ 😐 ☹ 😖

ENERGY LEVEL

ACTIVITIES

TODAY I WAS ANXIOUS ABOUT...
_____
_____
_____

❀ THREE POSITIVE THINGS ABOUT MY DAY WERE:

1. _____
2. _____
3. _____

FOOD INTAKE

JOURNAL ENTRY/FREE SPACE...

DATE: _____ S M T W T F S   HOURS SLEPT: _____

Morning Mood
☺ ☺ 😐 🙁 ☹

Energy Level

Activities

Goal for today...
♡ _____
♡♡ _____
♡♡♡ _____

❀ Three things I am grateful for....
1. _____
2. _____
3. _____

Food Intake
_____
_____
_____

Journal Entry/Free Space...

· + ✱ · ✺ ✻ ❋ o ✱ ☀ ✱ o ✺ ✱ · ✱ + ·

Evening Mood
☺ ☺ 😐 🙁 ☹

Energy Level

Activities

Today I was anxious about...
_____
_____

❀ Three positive things about my day were:
1. _____
2. _____
3. _____

Food Intake
_____
_____
_____

Journal Entry/Free Space...

DATE: _____ S M T W T F S   HOURS SLEPT: _____

MORNING MOOD

😊 🙂 😐 🙁 😟

ENERGY LEVEL

ACTIVITIES

♡ GOAL FOR TODAY... _____
♡♡ _____
♡♡♡ _____

❋ THREE THINGS I AM GRATEFUL FOR....

1. _____
2. _____
3. _____

FOOD INTAKE

JOURNAL ENTRY/FREE SPACE...

· + ✱ · ✲ ✱ ○ ✳ ✺ ✱ ○ ✱ ✱ · ✱ + ·

EVENING MOOD

😊 🙂 😐 🙁 😟

ENERGY LEVEL

ACTIVITIES

TODAY I WAS ANXIOUS ABOUT...
_____
_____

❋ THREE POSITIVE THINGS ABOUT MY DAY WERE:

1. _____
2. _____
3. _____

FOOD INTAKE

JOURNAL ENTRY/FREE SPACE...

DATE: _____ S M T W T F S   HOURS SLEPT: _____

MORNING MOOD
☺ ☺ 😐 🙁 ☹

ENERGY LEVEL

ACTIVITIES

GOAL FOR TODAY...
♡ _____
♡♡ _____
♡♡♡ _____

❀ THREE THINGS I AM GRATEFUL FOR....
1. _____
2. _____
3. _____

FOOD INTAKE

JOURNAL ENTRY/FREE SPACE...

· + ✸ · ✱ ✱ ○ ✱ ✸ ✱ ○ ✱ ★ · ✱ ✢ ·

EVENING MOOD
☺ ☺ 😐 🙁 ☹

ENERGY LEVEL

ACTIVITIES

TODAY I WAS ANXIOUS ABOUT...
_____
_____

❀ THREE POSITIVE THINGS ABOUT MY DAY WERE:
1. _____
2. _____
3. _____

FOOD INTAKE

JOURNAL ENTRY/FREE SPACE...

DATE: ―――――――― S M T W T F S   HOURS SLEPT: ――――――

MORNING MOOD

😊 🙂 😐 🙁 ☹

ENERGY LEVEL

ACTIVITIES

♡ GOAL FOR TODAY...
♡♡ ―――――――――――
♡♡♡ ―――――――――――

❋ THREE THINGS I AM GRATEFUL FOR....

1. ―――――――――――――――――――――――
2. ―――――――――――――――――――――――
3. ―――――――――――――――――――――――

FOOD INTAKE

JOURNAL ENTRY/FREE SPACE...

· ✦ ✱ · ✦ ✱ ○ ✱ ☀ ✱ ○ ✱ ✦ · ✱ ✦ ·

EVENING MOOD

😊 🙂 😐 🙁 ☹

ENERGY LEVEL

ACTIVITIES

TODAY I WAS ANXIOUS ABOUT...
―――――――――――――――――
―――――――――――――――――

❋ THREE POSITIVE THINGS ABOUT MY DAY WERE:

1. ―――――――――――――――――――――――
2. ―――――――――――――――――――――――
3. ―――――――――――――――――――――――

FOOD INTAKE

JOURNAL ENTRY/FREE SPACE...

DATE: _____ S M T W T F S   HOURS SLEPT: _____

MORNING MOOD

☺ ☺ ☺ ☹ ☹

ENERGY LEVEL

ACTIVITIES

GOAL FOR TODAY...
♡ _____
♡♡ _____
♡♡♡ _____

❀ THREE THINGS I AM GRATEFUL FOR....
1. _____
2. _____
3. _____

FOOD INTAKE

JOURNAL ENTRY/FREE SPACE...

· + ✱ · ✦ ✱ o ✱ ✺ ✱ o ✱ ✦ · ✱ + ·

EVENING MOOD

☺ ☺ ☺ ☹ ☹

ENERGY LEVEL

ACTIVITIES

TODAY I WAS ANXIOUS ABOUT...
_____
_____
_____

❀ THREE POSITIVE THINGS ABOUT MY DAY WERE:
1. _____
2. _____
3. _____

FOOD INTAKE

JOURNAL ENTRY/FREE SPACE...

DATE: _____ S M T W T F S   HOURS SLEPT: _____

MORNING MOOD

😊 🙂 😐 🙁 ☹️

ENERGY LEVEL
_____
_____
_____

ACTIVITIES

♡ GOAL FOR TODAY... _____
♡♡ _____
♡♡♡ _____

❋ THREE THINGS I AM GRATEFUL FOR....

1. _____
2. _____
3. _____

FOOD INTAKE
_____
_____
_____
_____

JOURNAL ENTRY/FREE SPACE...

. + ✱ • ✲ ✳ ○ ✶ ☀ ✴ ○ ✲ ✱ • ✳ + .

EVENING MOOD

😊 🙂 😐 🙁 ☹️

ENERGY LEVEL
_____
_____
_____

ACTIVITIES

TODAY I WAS ANXIOUS ABOUT...
_____
_____

❋ THREE POSITIVE THINGS ABOUT MY DAY WERE:

1. _____
2. _____
3. _____

FOOD INTAKE
_____
_____
_____
_____

JOURNAL ENTRY/FREE SPACE...

DATE: _____ S M T W T F S   HOURS SLEPT: _____

MORNING MOOD
😊 🙂 😐 🙁 ☹️

ENERGY LEVEL
_____
_____
_____

ACTIVITIES

♡ GOAL FOR TODAY... _____
♡♡ _____
♡♡♡ _____

❀ THREE THINGS I AM GRATEFUL FOR....
1. _____
2. _____
3. _____

FOOD INTAKE
_____
_____
_____
_____

JOURNAL ENTRY/FREE SPACE...

· + ✱ • ✳ · ✱ ○ ✱ ✺ ✱ ○ ✱ ★ • ✱ + ·

EVENING MOOD
😊 🙂 😐 🙁 ☹️

ENERGY LEVEL
_____
_____
_____

ACTIVITIES

TODAY I WAS ANXIOUS ABOUT...
_____
_____
_____

❀ THREE POSITIVE THINGS ABOUT MY DAY WERE:
1. _____
2. _____
3. _____

FOOD INTAKE
_____
_____
_____
_____

JOURNAL ENTRY/FREE SPACE...

DATE: _____ S M T W T F S   HOURS SLEPT: _____

MORNING MOOD

😀 🙂 😐 🙁 ☹️

ENERGY LEVEL

ACTIVITIES

GOAL FOR TODAY...
♡ _____
♡♡ _____
♡♡♡ _____

❋ THREE THINGS I AM GRATEFUL FOR....
1. _____
2. _____
3. _____

FOOD INTAKE

JOURNAL ENTRY/FREE SPACE...

EVENING MOOD

😀 🙂 😐 🙁 ☹️

ENERGY LEVEL

ACTIVITIES

TODAY I WAS ANXIOUS ABOUT...
_____
_____

❋ THREE POSITIVE THINGS ABOUT MY DAY WERE:
1. _____
2. _____
3. _____

FOOD INTAKE

JOURNAL ENTRY/FREE SPACE...

DATE: _____ S M T W T F S   HOURS SLEPT: _____

MORNING MOOD

😊 🙂 😐 🙁 ☹️

ENERGY LEVEL
_____
_____
_____

ACTIVITIES

GOAL FOR TODAY...
♡ _____
♡♡ _____
♡♡♡ _____

❀ THREE THINGS I AM GRATEFUL FOR....
1. _____
2. _____
3. _____

FOOD INTAKE
_____
_____
_____

JOURNAL ENTRY/FREE SPACE...

· + ✳ • ✱ ✳ ○ ✶ ☀ ✶ ○ ✳ ✱ • ✳ + ·

EVENING MOOD

😊 🙂 😐 🙁 ☹️

ENERGY LEVEL
_____
_____
_____

ACTIVITIES

TODAY I WAS ANXIOUS ABOUT...
_____
_____
_____

❀ THREE POSITIVE THINGS ABOUT MY DAY WERE:
1. _____
2. _____
3. _____

FOOD INTAKE
_____
_____
_____
_____

JOURNAL ENTRY/FREE SPACE...

DATE: _____ S M T W T F S   HOURS SLEPT: _____

MORNING MOOD

😊 🙂 😐 🙁 ☹️

ENERGY LEVEL
_____
_____
_____

ACTIVITIES

GOAL FOR TODAY...
♡ _____
♡♡ _____
♡♡♡ _____

❀ THREE THINGS I AM GRATEFUL FOR....
1. _____
2. _____
3. _____

FOOD INTAKE
_____
_____
_____

JOURNAL ENTRY/FREE SPACE...

· + ❋ · ✳ ❋ ○ ❋ ☀ ✺ ○ ❋ ✦ · ❋ ✚ ·

EVENING MOOD

😊 🙂 😐 🙁 ☹️

ENERGY LEVEL
_____
_____
_____

ACTIVITIES

TODAY I WAS ANXIOUS ABOUT...
_____
_____
_____

❀ THREE POSITIVE THINGS ABOUT MY DAY WERE:
1. _____
2. _____
3. _____

FOOD INTAKE
_____
_____
_____

JOURNAL ENTRY/FREE SPACE...

DATE: _____ S M T W T F S   HOURS SLEPT: _____

MORNING MOOD

😊 😀 😐 🙁 ☹️

ENERGY LEVEL

ACTIVITIES

♡ GOAL FOR TODAY...
♡♡ _____
♡♡♡ _____

❋ THREE THINGS I AM GRATEFUL FOR....
1. _____
2. _____
3. _____

FOOD INTAKE

JOURNAL ENTRY/FREE SPACE...

· + ✷ · ✱ ✶ ✴ ○ ✱ ✺ ✹ ○ ✷ ✱ · ✶ + ·

EVENING MOOD

😊 😀 😐 🙁 ☹️

ENERGY LEVEL

ACTIVITIES

TODAY I WAS ANXIOUS ABOUT...
_____
_____
_____

❋ THREE POSITIVE THINGS ABOUT MY DAY WERE:
1. _____
2. _____
3. _____

FOOD INTAKE

JOURNAL ENTRY/FREE SPACE...

DATE: —————— S M T W T F S   HOURS SLEPT: ——————

MORNING MOOD
😊 🙂 😐 🙁 ☹️

ENERGY LEVEL

ACTIVITIES

GOAL FOR TODAY...
♡ ——————————————
♡♡ ——————————————
♡♡♡ ——————————————

❀ THREE THINGS I AM GRATEFUL FOR....
1. ——————————————
2. ——————————————
3. ——————————————

FOOD INTAKE

JOURNAL ENTRY/FREE SPACE...

· ✦ * • ✱ ✳ ○ ✲ 🎆 ✹ ○ ✳ ✦ • ✱ ✦ ·

EVENING MOOD
😊 🙂 😐 🙁 ☹️

ENERGY LEVEL

ACTIVITIES

TODAY I WAS ANXIOUS ABOUT...
——————————————
——————————————

❀ THREE POSITIVE THINGS ABOUT MY DAY WERE:
1. ——————————————
2. ——————————————
3. ——————————————

FOOD INTAKE

JOURNAL ENTRY/FREE SPACE...

DATE: _____ S M T W T F S   HOURS SLEPT: _____

MORNING MOOD

😊 😀 😐 🙁 ☹️

ENERGY LEVEL
_____
_____
_____

ACTIVITIES

♡ GOAL FOR TODAY... _____
♡♡ _____
♡♡♡ _____

❁ THREE THINGS I AM GRATEFUL FOR....

1. _____
2. _____
3. _____

FOOD INTAKE
_____
_____
_____

JOURNAL ENTRY/FREE SPACE...

· + ✱ · ● · ❋ · ✱ ☀ ✱ ○ ✱ ★ · ❋ + ·

EVENING MOOD

😊 😀 😐 🙁 ☹️

ENERGY LEVEL
_____
_____
_____

ACTIVITIES

TODAY I WAS ANXIOUS ABOUT...
_____
_____
_____

❁ THREE POSITIVE THINGS ABOUT MY DAY WERE:

1. _____
2. _____
3. _____

FOOD INTAKE
_____
_____
_____

JOURNAL ENTRY/FREE SPACE...

DATE: ———————— S M T W T F S   HOURS SLEPT: ———————

MORNING MOOD

😀 🙂 😐 🙁 😟

ENERGY LEVEL

♡ GOAL FOR TODAY...
♡♡ ————————————————
♡♡♡ ————————————————

ACTIVITIES

❋ THREE THINGS I AM GRATEFUL FOR....

1. ————————————————
2. ————————————————
3. ————————————————

FOOD INTAKE

JOURNAL ENTRY/FREE SPACE...

EVENING MOOD

😀 🙂 😐 🙁 😟

ENERGY LEVEL

TODAY I WAS ANXIOUS ABOUT...
————————————————
————————————————

ACTIVITIES

❋ THREE POSITIVE THINGS ABOUT MY DAY WERE:

1. ————————————————
2. ————————————————
3. ————————————————

FOOD INTAKE

JOURNAL ENTRY/FREE SPACE...

DATE: _____ S M T W T F S   HOURS SLEPT: _____

MORNING MOOD
😊 🙂 😐 🙁 ☹️

ENERGY LEVEL
_____
_____
_____

ACTIVITIES

GOAL FOR TODAY...
♡ _____
♡♡ _____
♡♡♡ _____

❋ THREE THINGS I AM GRATEFUL FOR....
1. _____
2. _____
3. _____

FOOD INTAKE
_____
_____
_____
_____

JOURNAL ENTRY/FREE SPACE...

· + ❋ · ❋ ❋ ○ ❋ ☀ ❋ ○ ❋ ❋ · ❋ + ·

EVENING MOOD
😊 🙂 😐 🙁 ☹️

ENERGY LEVEL
_____
_____
_____

ACTIVITIES

TODAY I WAS ANXIOUS ABOUT...
_____
_____
_____

❋ THREE POSITIVE THINGS ABOUT MY DAY WERE:
1. _____
2. _____
3. _____

FOOD INTAKE
_____
_____
_____
_____

JOURNAL ENTRY/FREE SPACE...

DATE: _____ S M T W T F S   HOURS SLEPT: _____

MORNING MOOD

😊 🙂 😐 🙁 ☹

ENERGY LEVEL
_____
_____
_____

ACTIVITIES

♡ GOAL FOR TODAY...
_____
♡♡ _____
♡♡♡ _____

❊ THREE THINGS I AM GRATEFUL FOR....

1. _____
2. _____
3. _____

FOOD INTAKE
_____
_____
_____
_____

JOURNAL ENTRY/FREE SPACE...

· ✢ ✱ · ✦ ✱ ○ ✱ ✺ ✳ ○ ✱ ✱ · ✱ ✢ ·

EVENING MOOD

😊 🙂 😐 🙁 ☹

ENERGY LEVEL
_____
_____
_____

ACTIVITIES

TODAY I WAS ANXIOUS ABOUT...
_____
_____
_____

❊ THREE POSITIVE THINGS ABOUT MY DAY WERE:

1. _____
2. _____
3. _____

FOOD INTAKE
_____
_____
_____
_____

JOURNAL ENTRY/FREE SPACE...

DATE: _____ S M T W T F S   HOURS SLEPT: _____

MORNING MOOD

😊 🙂 😐 🙁 ☹️

ENERGY LEVEL
_____
_____
_____

ACTIVITIES

♡ GOAL FOR TODAY... _____
♡♡ _____
♡♡♡ _____

❊ THREE THINGS I AM GRATEFUL FOR....

1. _____
2. _____
3. _____

FOOD INTAKE
_____
_____
_____

JOURNAL ENTRY/FREE SPACE...

· ✢ ✻ · ✸ ✻ ○ ✻ ☀ ✷ ○ ✶ ✱ · ✻ ✢ ·

EVENING MOOD

😊 🙂 😐 🙁 ☹️

ENERGY LEVEL
_____
_____
_____

ACTIVITIES

TODAY I WAS ANXIOUS ABOUT...
_____
_____
_____

❊ THREE POSITIVE THINGS ABOUT MY DAY WERE:

1. _____
2. _____
3. _____

FOOD INTAKE
_____
_____
_____

JOURNAL ENTRY/FREE SPACE...

DATE: _____ S M T W T F S   HOURS SLEPT: _____

MORNING MOOD
😊 🙂 😐 🙁 ☹️

ENERGY LEVEL
_____
_____
_____

ACTIVITIES

GOAL FOR TODAY...
♡ _____
♡♡ _____
♡♡♡ _____

❋ THREE THINGS I AM GRATEFUL FOR....
1. _____
2. _____
3. _____

FOOD INTAKE
_____
_____
_____

JOURNAL ENTRY/FREE SPACE...

· ✛ ✱ · ✱ ✱ ○ ✱ ✺ ✶ ○ ✱ ✱ · ✱ ✛ ·

EVENING MOOD
😊 🙂 😐 🙁 ☹️

ENERGY LEVEL
_____
_____
_____

ACTIVITIES

TODAY I WAS ANXIOUS ABOUT...
_____
_____

❋ THREE POSITIVE THINGS ABOUT MY DAY WERE:
1. _____
2. _____
3. _____

FOOD INTAKE
_____
_____
_____

JOURNAL ENTRY/FREE SPACE...

DATE: _____ S M T W T F S HOURS SLEPT: _____

MORNING MOOD
☺ ☺ 😐 ☹ ☹

ENERGY LEVEL
_____
_____
_____

ACTIVITIES

♡ GOAL FOR TODAY... _____
♡♡ _____
♡♡♡ _____

❀ THREE THINGS I AM GRATEFUL FOR....
1. _____
2. _____
3. _____

FOOD INTAKE
_____
_____
_____
_____

JOURNAL ENTRY/FREE SPACE...

· + ✱ · ★ ✱ o ✱ ☀ ✱ o ✱ ★ · ✱ + ·

EVENING MOOD
☺ ☺ 😐 ☹ ☹

ENERGY LEVEL
_____
_____
_____

ACTIVITIES

TODAY I WAS ANXIOUS ABOUT...
_____
_____
_____

❀ THREE POSITIVE THINGS ABOUT MY DAY WERE:
1. _____
2. _____
3. _____

FOOD INTAKE
_____
_____
_____
_____

JOURNAL ENTRY/FREE SPACE...

Made in the USA
Columbia, SC
03 June 2025